FOLKLORE IN NIGERIAN LITERATURE

Folklore in Nigerian Literature

BERNTH LINDFORS

 Africana Publishing Company · New York

Published in the United States of America 1973 by
Africana Publishing Company, a Division of
Holmes & Meier Publishers, Inc.
101 Fifth Avenue, New York, N.Y. 10003

Great Britain:
Holmes & Meier Publishers, Ltd.
Hillview House
1, Hallswelle Parade
Finchley Road, London N.W. 11

Library of Congress Catalog Card Number: 72–91804
ISBN 0–8419–0134–1

Excerpts from *Arrow of God* by Chinua Achebe, © Chinua Achebe
1964, are reprinted by permission of William Heinemann Ltd. and
The John Day Company, Inc.

Excerpts from *The Palm-Wine Drinkard* by Amos Tutuola, © 1953
by George Braziller, are reprinted by permission of Faber and Faber
Ltd. and Grove Press, Inc.

Essays in this volume have appeared previously, as indicated, in the
following journals:
"Approaches to Folklore in African Literature," *The Conch*, 2, No. 2
(1970)
"Oral Tradition and the Individual Literary Talent," *Studies in the Novel*,
4 (1972)
"Amos Tutuola's *The Palm-Wine Drinkard* and Oral Tradition," *Critique*,
11 (1969)
"Amos Tutuola's Television-Handed Ghostess," *Ariel*, 2, No. 1 (1971)
"The Palm-Oil with Which Achebe's Words Are Eaten," *African Litera-
ture Today*, No. 1 (1968)
"The Folktale as Paradigm in Chinua Achebe's *Arrow of God*," *Studies in
Black Literature*, 1, No. 1 (1970)
"Wole Soyinka and the Horses of Speech," *Spectrum*, 3 (1973)
"Cyprian Ekwensi: An African Popular Novelist," *African Literature Today*,
No. 3 (1969)
"Heroes and Hero-Worship in Nigerian Chapbooks," *Journal of Popular
Culture*, 1, No. 1 (1967)

To
Judy, Brenda, Susan,
and Erik

ACKNOWLEDGMENTS

I wish to thank the editors of *African Literature Today, Ariel, Black Orpheus, The Conch, Critique, Journal of Popular Culture, Studies in Black Literature, Studies in the Novel,* and *Spectrum* for allowing me to reprint essays which first appeared in their pages. I also wish to thank Sunday Anozie, Barbara Kirschenblatt-Gimblett and Kathleen McCarthy for reading the manuscript of this book and making suggestions which have led to a number of revisions.

CONTENTS

INTRODUCTION

The white critic of black literature has become a controversial figure in recent years, especially in the United States. Many articulate, young Afro-American intellectuals have begun to insist that "despite the proliferation of 'experts,' whites are unable to evaluate the Black Experience, and, consequently, any work of art derived from it or addressed to those who live it."[1] Whites should therefore abandon the field to blacks, who are innately better qualified to understand and appreciate their own literature.

A similar argument has been voiced in Nigeria by authors and critics who feel that African literary works have often been grossly misinterpreted by foreigners with little or no first-hand acquaintance with African life. Chinua Achebe once complained of "getting a little weary of all the special types of criticism which have been designed for us by people whose knowledge of us is very limited."[2] J. P. Clark also spoke out against the "smug patronage or outrage some [expatriate] critics have shown" because of their "jaundice of prejudice" against African writers who dare to say things whites do not want to hear.[3] More recently Ernest Emenyonu has asserted that "what many Western critics issue on African literature is a reflection of a profound lack of knowledge about African cultural traditions coupled with an ignorance of the existence, nature and depth of the heritage of African oral literature. In most cases some vague literary background or a landing on an African soil has not been enough to correct this intellectual imbalance."[4] While these statements condemning the incompetence of white critics are not as extreme as those heard in America today, they do point in the same racial direction: black critics are acclaimed as the best possible interpreters of their own literature.

The standard reply to these views has been that no race can claim a monopoly on critical sensitivity and that those who advocate esthetic apartheid are only painting themselves into a dark corner. A favorite tactic is to reverse the argument by asking "Should all the black critics—and this includes Africans as well as Afro-Americans and teachers and professors of literature throughout the world—be given a similar 'hands off' ultimatum on non-black writing?"[5] An affirmative answer to this question would be very hard to justify.

There is, of course, a measure of truth on each side of the debate. Bearers of a culture *are* better equipped to interpret that culture than aliens who have experienced its realities only vicariously. Those who share a writer's background *can* more readily comprehend the full implications of his message. Yet accomplished works of art communicate in such a universal human idiom that they are capable of transcending their particular time and place and speaking to all mankind. One does not have to be Greek to understand Homer, Hindu to appreciate Kalidasa, or Japanese to enjoy Chikamatsu. So why should a person have to be black to respond to James Baldwin, George Lamming or Amos Tutuola?

Actually, Afro-American critics are usually among the first to admit that they do not possess any special qualifications for interpreting African literature. They may feel a close kinship or rapport with Africans, but they realize this alone will not help them to penetrate the Africanness of a poem by Christopher Okigbo or a play by Wole Soyinka. Like other outsiders, they know they must conscientiously study an African writer's background and culture before trying to decipher the subtle nuances of meaning which may reside in his work. Without such research their appreciation of African literary accomplishments will remain as limited as that of any other foreign reader. They will be so lost in the awesome forest of universals that they will fail to recognize the distinctiveness of the individual black trees that surround them.

The essays in this book are attempts by one non-African

reader to examine the artistic functions of native folklore in modern Nigerian literature in English. I define folklore in its broadest sense to include popular beliefs, stereotypes and verbal performance styles as well as folktales, proverbs and other forms of patterned oral art. Some folklorists might object to the presence of essays on popular culture and rhetoric in a book of this sort, but I would defend their inclusion by pointing out that I deal with these subjects in the same way that I deal with others. My primary focus is always on the impact of traditions of verbal expression on the written word, and I am particularly interested in the skill with which Nigerian writers exploit new esthetic opportunities by incorporating traditional matter in the novels, plays and poems they write in a language which is not their mother tongue. I believe that those who do this most successfully are contributing something original to world literature.

Although I have been a student of African literature for more than a decade, I can claim no special expertise in African folkways and no extraordinary insight into characteristic modes of African thought, traditional or modern. Much of what I say in these essays is speculative and open to challenge, but I have tried to avoid making statements which cannot be supported by solid evidence from the literature itself. Like any traveller in a strange new land, I have looked for reliable guideposts, sought directions, drawn crude maps, and kept out of those areas where I suspected I might not be welcome or feared I might lose my way. I have made an effort to go as far as an outsider can go in a culture he knows mainly through books, and if my meanderings stimulate others—insiders as well as outsiders—to go further and draw better maps, I will feel the journey has been worthwhile.

A word of warning: Since these essays were written at intervals over a period of five or six years, they are not always consistent with one another or with the principles advocated in the first two essays, which were written last. Indeed, the advice I offer to critics of African literature in the section on "Critical Perspectives" is the result of hindsight, of learning through my own blunders the pitfalls a critic should seek to avoid. If the reader expects my own criticism to live up to the high principles I espouse for others, I am afraid he is likely to be disappointed. And if he anticipates that each essay will be organically connected to those that precede and follow it, then he surely will be dismayed by the loose grab bag of ideas he finds here. For these are essays in the older sense of the word—"trials, attempts, experiments in learning"—and each was originally intended to stand alone. They have been brought together here because they all seek to define the impact of oral tradition on the emergence of a literary tradition in English in Nigeria.

But though the main emphasis is on the influence that one type of verbal art has had upon another, it is hoped that those who are searching for evidence of the African personality of this literature will find something here to satisfy them. Each essay was written to prove a particular point, but together they tend to affirm that much African writing, even when done in a foreign language and a Western literary form, remains indelibly African in cultural orientation and style. At least I would like to think the essays affirm this. In exploring a relatively new field, I have tried to distinguish some of the idiosyncrasies of local cultivation without losing sight of the vast common ground from which all living art draws its primary strength.

Whether I have succeeded or failed is for others to judge. If I have made any egregious errors or committed any sins of cultural misinterpretation, I have no one to blame but myself. The Ibos have a saying that a man who brings ant-ridden faggots into his hut should expect the visit of lizards. If I have brought in anything unsound, I hope sharp-tongued critics will descend on me and demolish my ideas, not because I am white but because I am wrong.

B.L.

AUSTIN, TEXAS, JULY 1972

NOTES

1 Mercer Cook and Stephen E. Henderson, *The Militant Black Writer in Africa and the United States* (Madison, 1969), p. 79.
2 Chinua Achebe, "Where Angels Fear to Tread," *Nigeria Magazine*, No. 75 (1962), p. 61.
3 J. P. Clark, "Our Literary Critics," *Nigeria Magazine*, No. 74 (1962), p. 80.
4 Ernest Emenyonu, "African literature: What does it take to be its critic?," *African Literature Today*, No. 5 (1971), pp. 9–10.
5 Charles R. Larson, review of Cook and Henderson book, *Research in African Literatures*, 1, No. 1 (1970), p. 106.

APPROACHES TO FOLKLORE IN AFRICAN LITERATURE

Reading criticism of contemporary African literature is rather like taking a quick sight-seeing tour over much of the continent. In several places one finds vast, uninteresting, arid stretches barren of living ideas. In others there are dense rain forests—dark, mysterious, almost impenetrable, but impressively canopied with large, umbrella-like metaphysical speculations. Then there are the oozing swamps and marshes where slippery hypotheses and dangerous assumptions lurk. Naturally, not all the landscape is this depressing. One also notices a few well-cultivated highlands, one or two mountain peaks of truly lofty elevation, and scattered diamond fields and gold mines capable of yielding great riches if properly exploited. But most of the terrain is a bleak grassland tedious to traverse, unrewarding to excavate, and likely to infect even the thickest-skinned traveller with sleeping sickness. Literary criticism remains the most underdeveloped of African arts.

One reason it has remained so is that the majority of the practitioners of this art have not been themselves Africans. They have been foreigners—mostly Europeans and Americans—trying to cope with world views different from their own. Some have had outstanding credentials as professors of literature or anthropology, as long-term residents of Africa, or as lifetime students of African culture. And several have been very serious about their work, even to the extent of sacrificing a number of personal comforts in order to undertake difficult, painstaking research "in the field." Yet like obstetricians or voyeurs, they have always stood outside looking in, observers rather than participants in the creative process that absorbs so much of their attention and yet is alien to their own cultural

experience. They have not been unhelpful, some of these wit-
nesses. A few have done a great deal to encourage and publicize
the birth of new literatures in Africa. Others have watched these
infants grow, commenting on salient trends in their development. Such discreet spectators do not offend their hosts. But
there are sensitive zones—the inner sanctuaries and sacred
groves—which are closed to strangers and accessible only to
those within a society who have grown up learning the pass-
words. "No man," Chinua Achebe has said, "can understand
another whose language he does not speak." And by "language"
Achebe meant not simply words but "a man's entire world-
view."[1] Foreign critics should heed this warning and not attempt to trespass brazenly on territory that belongs to others
who acquired the indigenous grammar while young and thus
know how to decode and interpret the deep structures underlying their own semantic universe.

I am not arguing that there is no place for the non-African
critic of African letters, only that he should know his place.
Obviously, there are jobs he is competent to do and skills he
brings to his work which are productive of good results. But if he
tries to enter one of the sensitive zones, he should recognize his
own limitations, fortify himself with every scrap of cultural
information he can find, and then inch very warily but imagina-
tively into the arena. He may not get far—indeed, he may make
no real progress at all—but at least he will have shown his
respect for someone else's ancestral grounds. And he will have
demonstrated by his lack of pretentiousness that he is not an
ignorant interloper rushing in where even minor deities fear to
tread.

One of the most sensitive areas of African literary research,
and one of the most abused and neglected, is that in which
investigators search for evidence of folklore in the literature.
The evidence is not difficult to find, but the uses to which it is
put vary so greatly that it may be helpful to pause here to construct a crude typology of the species and subspecies of this
genus of criticism so that the distinctive features of each type

[7]

may be better isolated and identified. There appear to be three basic critical approaches to folklore in African literature: the impressionistic, the anthropological, and the interpretative. These may be arranged in a hierarchy with "impressionistic" at the bottom and "interpretative" at the top, for each successive level seems to require a greater degree of critical sophistication and cultural expertise. Each category may also be subdivided by quality—i.e., from bad to good—with the best items in one category standing higher than the worst items in the next category up the ladder. There is some overlap in the hierarchy, in other words. Impressionists are not necessarily intrinsically inferior to anthropologists and interpreters. Their rank in the scale would depend to a large degree on the quality of their work. There are also some crossbreeds—impressionistic anthropologists and anthropological interpreters—who blur the diagram still further, but most critics can be pigeonholed quite neatly in one of the three major categories.

Let us begin with the impressionists. An impressionistic approach to folklore in African literature is one involving assumptions and suggestions rather than facts and proofs. The critic is content to make a few bland assertions about the presence of traditional elements in a modern literary work without bothering to ascertain whether what he says about these elements is true. This kind of critic does not like to take the trouble to do research. He prefers merely to read a work, react to it, and then record his reactions. If he happens to notice that Amos Tutuola makes use of folktales in his fiction or that Wole Soyinka's characters frequently speak in proverbs, he might draw attention to the phenomenon and offer the opinion that these tales or proverbs are undoubtedly "traditional among the Yoruba." No verification is necessary. The mere fact that the thought has crossed the critic's mind is enough justification for preserving it in print. Such criticism, needless to say, is superficial and highly unreliable.

Examples of this kind of criticism can be found in abundance in Anne Tibble's book *African/English Literature*.[2] Her discussion of Tutuola's use of oral tradition is almost as garbled as the adventures of one of Tutuola's heroes. "The quest Tutuola tells of [in *The Palm-Wine Drinkard*]," she says, "incorporates fantasies that most of us as children encountered in dream and daydream or in legends. Legends would include Biblical myth, heroic myth, Greek, and north-European myth. Mingled with these are myths of a lurid Africa partly of Tutuola's fervent imagination, partly of his knowledge of Yoruba oral folk-tales." Besides mangling the professional folklorist's nice distinctions between myth, legend and folktale as forms of narrative, Tibble here makes immense assumptions about both Tutuola's heritage and the average reader's childhood. I want it known that I for one cannot truthfully say that I have ever met any of Tutuola's bizarre freaks and monsters in my dreams, daydreams or readings of the Bible, Homer, Hans Christian Andersen or the brothers Grimm. How Anne Tibble arrived at her supposed omniscience about me—much less Tutuola—is indeed bewildering!

However, she goes on to qualify her sweeping generalizations with the following statement: "None of these types of myth can properly be called universal, as sometimes Tutuola's myths are claimed to be. Present knowledge of world myths is not sufficient to pronounce universality for any. But many undoubtedly are common to a variety of cultures." Now she is on somewhat safer ground, and she continues by drawing a number of parallels. Tutuola's "Faithful-Mother in the White Tree," for instance, is shown to have "Asian, African, and European" affinities, being comparable to "Graves's White Goddess, the earth-mother of Northern myth, the Mother Goddesses of Hindu villages, and of many another culture myth or religious myth. Her White Tree is comparable with the sacred Bo Tree, Igdrazil, the Druid's oak, the Tree of Knowledge, the Tree of Life. The swallowing of the Drinkard and his wife by the Hungry Creature, and the Drinkard's hacking his way out of Hungry Creature's stomach reminds us of Jonah and the Whale." These analogies are valid and interesting as analogies, but they are not proof that Tutuola borrowed his motifs from Şcandinavian, Greek, Jewish or Hindu mythology. Tibble unfortunately falls into the trap of actually regarding some of these fortuitous analogues as genuine sources of inspiration for Tutuola. "The last chapter of *The Palm-Wine Drinkard*," she says, "shows Tutuola using a final blend of African and European myth." And "if there is a falling-off between his first book and his later books that is solely because there isn't a sufficient number of Afro-European myths to use effectively twice." Statements like these reveal that Tibble has been hoist with her own petard.

Despite her shortcomings as a comparative mythologist, it must be conceded that Tibble at least knows something about oral tradition and tries to relate what she knows to African literature. The same cannot be said of most other impressionistic critics, whose total contribution to this branch of African literary study consists of offhand remarks unsupported by even the tiniest shred of evidence. John Povey has developed the habit of tossing off comments like "the story of *Lion and the Jewel* is common enough, a constant theme of many folk tales"[3] and "Soyinka's own *A Dance of the Forests* is developed from the Yoruba Egungun Festival,"[4] but these interesting tidbits of literary gossip are never authenticated, never elaborated, never even adequately thought out. Since Povey holds the view that "although [these] writers are African, it is more easily possible to seek out some link between their writing and the twentieth century western trends than the connection between their work and the traditional forms of African literature,"[5] perhaps he feels it would be unrewarding to pursue such matters further. Or perhaps he simply does not want to do the necessary homework. Of course, the real fault may lie in the very nature of impressionistic criticism itself, a kind of loose-tongued scholarship that allows the critic the luxury of making glib pronouncements about serious works of literary art.

Anthropological criticism is just the opposite. The anthropological critic who studies folklore in African literature tends to be obsessed with documentation. He wants to verify the legitimate ancestry of every item of folklore he comes across, tracing it back to published collections of oral data, to unpublished field notes, or to testimony from bearers of the culture from which it has supposedly emerged. Anthropological criticism can thus be viewed as a necessary and useful overcorrection of impressionistic criticism, but it has some limitations of its own which reduce its value as commentary on African literature. In a sense, it is an elaboration of the obvious, an illustration of an accepted truth, and as such, informative only to other outsiders. An essay which merely documents Chinua Achebe's use of traditional Ibo proverbs would tell an Ibo nothing that he did not already know. There may be a place for such criticism outside Africa, but the critics who practice it should beware of the danger of compiling data only for data's sake.

Two anthropological critics who go beyond elementary indexing of oral lore in African literature are Nancy Schmidt and Austin Shelton. Schmidt, in an essay entitled "Nigerian Fiction and the African Oral Tradition,"[6] examines the ways in which folktales, proverbs and praise names have influenced the narrative techniques of a great number of Nigerian short story writers and novelists. It is her contention that "even though the content of the fiction may bear little superficial resemblance to that of oral tradition . . . the primarily narrative nature of the fiction can be traced to [it], as can the use of proverbial references and praise names for description and the use of proverbs and tales for providing commentary on the actions of the characters." The argument is well illustrated and well documented, but it seldom ventures outside narrow formal considerations to wider matters of interpretation and evaluation of the artistic uses of oral tradition in Nigerian fiction. Nevertheless within its restricted compass, it is a job conscientiously done and a job that very much needed doing, since there were a number of impressionistic critics other than Povey who had not yet seen the light. Michael Crowder, for instance, had expressed the opinion that "there is no readily apparent continuity between the creative writing of modern Nigerian authors and the traditional literature of Nigeria. . . . Indeed one is tempted to believe that the two are of a totally different nature and that any link between them is either a fiction of the expatriate critic's imagination or merely fortuitous."[7] Schmidt's essay exposed this notion of a lack of continuity between Nigerian oral and written literatures as the real fiction of the expatriate critic's imagination.

Austin Shelton is perhaps the anthropological critic *par excellence*, for he is seldom content simply to annotate examples of oral influence on written literature. Instead he uses them to make responsible literary interpretations which are grounded on careful study of an author's culture. In this respect his work transcends that of most anthropological critics. He is an anthropological interpreter, not merely a compiler of lists or writer of footnotes. His essay on "The Articulation of Traditional and Modern in Igbo Literature"[8] surpasses Schmidt's in depth and range of insight, and his study of proverbs in Chinua Achebe's novels is a model of informed analysis.[9] Believing that "the ethnocentric application of European criteria of cultural and literary criticism to African writings" leads to false, misleading and irrelevant evaluations of these works,[10] he strives to remain faithful to African esthetic criteria in his own critical assessments. Though one might disagree with some of his interpretations[11] and wish at times that he would display more imagination in his exegeses of folklore-ridden literary texts, one must applaud his methods and admire his assiduity. He is an outsider who tries very hard to achieve an insider's point of view.

Having examined models of bad impressionistic criticism and good anthropological criticism, let us now move a step higher and view a few representative works by the best interpretative critics. Interpretative criticism concerns itself with establishing and defending a theoretical position upon a body of literature. It avoids careless overstatements and amasses data only when the data is useful to the argument being advanced. The interpretative critic who studies traditional elements in contemporary

African literature is more likely to be interested in investigating their artistic functions or their esthetic and metaphysical implications than in merely validating their existence. He seeks to go beyond the obvious into less accessible regions, sometimes even venturing to use his tools to probe the mysterious inner workings of the human mind. He is the most adventurous of all critics.

Gerald Moore is one of these. Though much of his early writing could be branded superior impressionism, he has recently published a few essays which reflect a maturity of thought unusual in African literary criticism. In "Time and Experience in African Poetry,"[12] he argues that in both traditional and modern African poetry "time seems often to be conceived simply as a projection from living experience, rather than as an abstract sequence of fixed units existing in its own right and imposing its pattern upon human activities. The activity itself is paramount, the time sequence relative and adaptable." Bolstering his case with examples from the traditional poetry of the Acholi, Lango and Yoruba, and from the modern poetry of Kofi Awoonor, Lenrie Peters, J. P. Clark and Tchicaya U Tam'si, Moore concludes by briefly surveying the cosmological beliefs of the Dogon and Dinka peoples, who also share this "dynamic conception of time." The strength of Moore's argument (which at first seems almost Janheinz Jahn-like in its facile acceptance of the notion of African "universals") lies in its wide range of reference. The examples are plucked from West, East, Central and Saharan Africa, and anthropologists of the stature of Marcel Griaule, Godfrey Lienhardt and John Beattie are called upon for testimony in support of the thesis. Moore has obviously prepared his case carefully.

In a second essay, this time on "The Imagery of Death in African Poetry,"[13] Moore again casts his net wide to illustrate his contention that African oral poetry and contemporary African poetry written in English and French share "a number of common themes in the imagery with which [they handle] the fact of death." The traditional examples are drawn primarily from the Acholi and Yoruba but a few fleeting references are made to the Ibo and Dogon. The modern examples come from the poems of Gabriel Okara, Wole Soyinka, Kofi Awoonor, Lenrie Peters, J. P. Clark, Valente Malangatana, Birago Diop, and Tchicaya U Tam'si. Moore's wide range of reference is again impressive, but one begins to wonder if a similar kind of eclecticism could not be used to prove an opposite point. If we were to select different tribes or different poets or even simply different poems from the same tribes and poets, would we necessarily have to come to the same conclusions as Moore does about time, experience and death? Although Moore's aim is to demonstrate a kind of pan-African unity of world view reflected through poetry, he might have made his case more convincing had he commenced by showing how some of the modern poets retain in their verse certain of the attitudes toward human experience which are traditional *among their own people* and expressed in poetry *in their own mother tongue.* The only point at which Moore comes close to this kind of tribalistic analysis is in his discussion of some of Wole Soyinka's works, which he appropriately relates to Yoruba tradition. Had he also taken pains to demonstrate that the poetry of Okara or Clark contains residual Ijaw-isms or that Awoonor is still wedded to an Ewe Muse, perhaps then he would have found it easier to take the reader along with him on his great leaps across the continent when he attempts to find correspondences between these poets and the funeral singers of Acholiland. Moore is a perceptive critic, but sometimes he asks the reader to accept too much in good faith.

Another interesting interpretative critic, who does the kind of work that Moore shirks, is Robert Plant Armstrong. In a splendid theoretical essay entitled "The Narrative and Intensive Continuity: *The Palm-Wine Drinkard*,"[14] Armstrong attempts to isolate those features of Tutuola's fiction which place it in the narrative tradition of the Yoruba. He bases his analysis on the assumption that

> one's method of telling a story is the same whether he does it in
> one language or in a very different one; he will assert metaphors

at the same kinds of places, similarly shape events, similarly pro-
portion them and invoke their relationships, and will even tailor
the second language somewhat—if he is not a master of its own
idiom—along the stylistic lines of that mother tongue he more perfectly knows, much as he will shape the sounds of a second language
to conform to the phonemes of his mother tongue.

Armstrong finds that the various "media" of Tutuola's narrative—situationality, language, relationality, and experience—
are characterized by what he calls "intensive continuity" and
that this dense, impacted, episodic mode of self-expression is
itself a hallmark of the Yoruba esthetic, one which is actualized
in Yoruba sculpture, painting, music, dance and other plastic
and performing arts as well as in traditional forms of oral narrative. Armstrong's strength lies in the elegance of his theoretical
construct and in the remarkable support he finds for his thesis
in the non-narrative arts. He is a comparative esthetician more
interested in philosophy than in folklore or literature *per se*, and
his obvious delight in building coherent systems of logical
abstractions gives his essay a heady elevation which, though
intellectually stimulating, is nonetheless a little disconcerting in
its spanking neatness of architecture, its seemingly strict adherence to a prefabricated design.

For the nagging questions persist. How valid are his underlying assumptions? How responsible his use of evidence? How
accurate his vision of the Yoruba arts? How wide his reading?
How comprehensive his knowledge of other African esthetic
systems? Can his ideas survive close scrutiny and rigorous ques-
tioning? Or is his a delicate theory which can be put to death by
an uncomfortable fact? These are the kinds of questions one is
tempted to ask anyone who dares to indulge in ambitious,
original scholarship. But in the cases of Armstrong and Moore,
the questions need answering, for only in such imaginative
interpretative criticism are important theoretical issues at stake.

Here is where the African critic can perform a valuable service. By exposing the faulty assumptions of his non-African
colleagues, by testing their theories against his own experience

of African verbal arts, by challenging or affirming their interpretations, he can help to weed out error and promote the
cultivation of truth. This is not to say that he should be content
with a second-class role as tenant farmer tending someone else's
crops. He must also plant seeds of his own after clearing the land
of worthless foreign brambles. And he must nurture his ideas
carefully so that they bear mature fruit. To do his work well, he
will probably need professional training in the fields of folklore,
anthropology and literature, but if he is sensitive to the needs
of the soil and quick to learn new techniques, he may become a
productive worker without serving a long apprenticeship. Since
this fertile new land is his birthright, he should now claim it and
take an interest in making it yield a rich harvest.

There is already some evidence that this is being done. The
writings of Michael Echeruo, Oyin Ogunba, Sunday Anozie
and others[15] are breaking fresh ground in the study of folklore in
African literature. These critics usually come to their tasks with
a distinct advantage over their European and American colleagues. Much of the cultural information which the non-
African critic must labor to acquire is already in their possession,
so they can proceed almost immediately to the higher levels of
analysis and interpretation. They are not strangers footloose in
an exotic Arcadia but natives who know their way about their
own ancestral lands.

Let us look at a few examples of what these critics have contributed to African literary studies. Michael Echeruo, an accomplished lyric poet, has given us one of the most perceptive
analyses of the use of traditional and borrowed elements in
modern Nigerian poetry. Examining four possible areas of influence—technique, delivery, subject matter, and the resources
of language—he points out that the contemporary Nigerian
poet who seeks to transfer traditional elements of oral vernacular
poetry into his own Anglophonic verse must first effect a compromise with the English language. Because he writes in a
foreign tongue, he will not be able to avoid a debt to foreign
poetry, for he immediately will be confronted with the problem

of translating "a local sensibility and an indigenous environment into an alien artifact: the English poem."[16] Both the poet and his message will have to seek the mediation of a non-African linguistic medium. Citing examples from the works of Christopher Okigbo, Wole Soyinka, J. P. Clark, Okogbule Nwanodi and many less famous Nigerian poets, Echeruo demonstrates how splendid or disastrous the results of such mediation can be. One of his most interesting bits of evidence is Okigbo's poem honoring Yeats, which is shown to be a variation on a traditional Ede praise song that Okigbo had read in English translation. Echeruo reveals that Okigbo, an Ibo poet, made decidedly literary use of this foreign African source, turning his own poem into an exercise in English centenary verse even while following quite closely the oral structure and imagery of the Ede original. He then goes on to examine one of Nwanodi's poems which, though more truly informed by the praise song tradition, does nothing to draw attention to its indebtedness and therefore succeeds in standing on its own as an independent creation. Echeruo concludes that "the process of identifying influences— whether from traditional or from foreign sources—requires an exacting and sensitive appreciation of the poem and the imaginative power of the poet. There is no other meaningful process."[17] One wonders, however, if this process would be quite so meaningful if the influences happened to be identified by someone knowing less about both cultures than Echeruo does. Echeruo's keen insights into the poetry of his contemporaries prove that a well-informed Nigerian critic whose education and upbringing have made him familiar with Western literary traditions as well as African oral traditions stands the best chance of clearly discerning the imaginative contribution of a Nigerian poet writing in English.

What Echeruo does for our understanding of Nigerian poetry, Oyin Ogunba, a Yoruba critic, does for our appreciation of the theatrical works of Wole Soyinka, a Yoruba dramatist who writes in English. In an essay on "The Traditional Content of the Plays of Wole Soyinka," Ogunba notes that the most significant traditional element in at least three of his plays is the "overall design of a festival."[18] *Kongi's Harvest* is modeled on a Yoruba king's festival, *The Strong Breed* on a purification festival, and *A Dance of the Forests*, his most complex work, on an "averted" Yoruba Egungun festival. Soyinka captures the appropriate festival mood in each of these plays but sometimes takes liberties with traditional structure, sequence and symbolism in order to reverse expectations ironically and make an original statement on human behavior. In *Kongi's Harvest*, for instance,

> [Soyinka] reverses the normal sequence of events in a Yoruba king's festival, making the triumphal dance precede the ritual dance and is thus able to emphasise the more the imminent extinction of tradition. The whole idea of the royal dance in tradition is to show in symbolic terms the process by which a régime passes through toil and occasional tragedies to the glory of the present. In so doing, the royal tradition is presented to the populace as a triumph of civilization. Almost invariably, such a dance features a progress through ritual reminiscent of the trials of state-building, to eventual success.
>
> In *Kongi's Harvest*, by contrast, the trials continue, and extinction is in sight; merriment evaporates, and despair and death descend on the traditional characters. The attempt to revive the dance and reenact the mood of joy and royal splendour in the Second Part, therefore, becomes an anti-climax and so warrants Daodu's tearing of the royal drum which gives a finale to the royal make-believe.[19]

Who but a critic totally immersed in Yoruba culture could have made such a point? Criticism like this illuminates not only the art of the play and the craft of the playwright but also the complex civilization from which both have emerged.

Echeruo and Ogunba are prime examples of African critics who serve as excellent anthropological interpreters. They are able to guide us through the intricacies of custom, ritual and song because they grew up as participants in the culture they explore. As native speakers of the total traditional grammar of self-expression, they are sensitive to nuances and ambiguities which the outsider would miss. They are masters, not students, of their society.

Not every African critic of African literature is anthropologically inclined, however. A few function on an entirely different plane, seeking to make theoretical statements which have universal validity as well as a special local relevance. One such interpretative critic is Sunday Anozie, a Sorbonne-trained Nigerian scholar who has almost singlehandedly pioneered the application of a new critical approach to African literature, a technique which he terms "genetic structuralism."[20] Based on the socio-literary theories of Lucien Goldmann and Georg Lukács, genetic structuralism eschews historical and nationalistic modes of literary inquiry in favor of a more rigorous sociological approach which examines various interplays between thematic and structural elements in literature. These interplays, or "genetic relationships," emerge from and reflect the social and cultural realities which produced the literature, yet they function independently as a separate but homologous dynamic system governed by its own internal laws of organic growth. Although genetic structuralism pays little attention to esthetic considerations, it does seek to treat every literature as an "autonomous field of discourse . . . capable of sustaining a specific and, also in a sense, an original world view." Anozie believes that

> if the description of all the objective, ascertainable elements that make up such a world view also leads, as in fact it should, to the identification of an original aesthetic system or structure, this new phenomenon will logically have confirmed our original hypothesis that, considered as a language or as a biological organism, every creative system is autonomous within its field of reference and action, but no system is finite if it can be shown that at least in one respect it forms part of a larger and autonomous creative system.[21]

Anozie has applied this method of criticism to West African fiction,[22] to the poetry of Christopher Okigbo,[23] and to African vernacular and oral literature,[24] and through his editing of *The Conch*, a biannual "Sociological Journal of African Cultures and Literatures" which he founded in Paris in 1969 and now publishes in New York, he has stimulated others to analyze structural dimensions of African creativity. In so doing, he has carried the study of folklore in African literature to new levels of profundity, advancing far beyond the surface manifestations of indigenous culture to the deeper realms of subconscious psychological and sociocultural awareness that characterize the African world view. He is one of the first and finest African interpretative critics of African literature.

With sophisticated native critics like Anozie, Echeruo and Ogunba beginning to emerge from universities at home and abroad, there is no need for anyone to worry about the future of African literary studies. Indeed, if such critics continue to develop their powers of observation and to explore hidden regions inaccessible to others, surely those of us who wish to take future excursions into African literature will find them the most reliable and exciting guides.

NOTES
1 Chinua Achebe, "Where Angels Fear to Tread," *Nigeria Magazine*, No. 75 (1962), p. 62.
2 Anne Tibble, *African/English Literature* (London, 1965). Quotations are taken from pages 96 to 98.
3 John Povey, "Wole Soyinka: Two Nigerian Comedies," *Comparative Drama*, 3, No. 2 (1969), 126.
4 John Povey, "Wole Soyinka and the Nigerian Drama," *Triquarterly*, No. 5 (1966), p. 129.
5 John Povey, "Canons of Criticism for Neo-African Literature," *Proceedings of a Conference on African Languages and Literatures Held at Northwestern University, April 28–30, 1966*, ed. Jack Berry *et al.* (n.p., n.d.), p. 73.
6 Nancy Schmidt, "Nigerian Fiction and the African Oral Tradition," *Journal of the New African Literature and the Arts*, No. 5/6 (1968), pp. 10–19.
7 Michael Crowder, "Tradition and Change in Nigerian Literature," *Triquarterly*, No. 5 (1966), p. 117.
8 Austin Shelton, "The Articulation of Traditional and Modern in Igbo Literature," *The Conch*, 1, No. 1 (1969), 30–52.

9 Austin Shelton, "The 'Palm-Oil' of Language: Proverbs in Chinua Achebe's Novels," *Modern Language Quarterly*, 30, No. 1 (1969), 86–111.
10 Austin Shelton, "Critical Criteria for the Study of African Literature," *Literature East and West*, 12, No. 1 (1968), 9.
11 An Ibo critic, Donatus Nwoga, has taken strong exception to his interpretation of the Ibo concept of *chi*. See Shelton's essay "The Offended *chi* in Achebe's Novels," *Transition*, No. 13 (1964), pp. 36–37, and Nwoga's reply, "The *chi* Offended," *Transition*, No. 15 (1964), p. 5.
12 Gerald Moore, "Time and Experience in African Poetry," *Transition*, No. 26 (1966), pp. 18–22.
13 Gerald Moore, "The Imagery of Death in African Poetry," *Africa*, 38 (1968), 57–70.
14 Robert Plant Armstrong, "The Narrative and Intensive Continuity: *The Palm-Wine Drinkard*," *Research in African Literatures*, 1, No. 1 (1970), 9–34.
15 See, e.g., Emmanuel Obiechina, "Transition from Oral to Literary Tradition," *Présence Africaine*, No. 63 (1967), pp. 140–61, and "Amos Tutuola and the Oral Tradition," *Présence Africaine*, No. 65 (1968), pp. 85–106; Ben Obumselu, "The Background of Modern African Literature," *Ibadan*, No. 22 (1966), pp. 46–59; J. A. Adedeji, "Oral Tradition and the Contemporary Theater in Nigeria," *Research in African Literatures*, 2, No. 2 (1971), 134–49; and Oyekan Owomoyela, "Folklore and Yoruba Theater," *Research in African Literatures*, 2, No. 2 (1971), 121–33.
16 Michael Echeruo, "Traditional and Borrowed Elements in Nigerian Poetry," *Nigeria Magazine*, No. 89 (1966), p. 143.
17 *Ibid.*, p. 145.
18 Oyin Ogunba, "The Traditional Content of the Plays of Wole Soyinka," *African Literature Today*, No. 4 (1970), p. 8. (This article is continued in *African Literature Today*, No. 5 (1971), pp. 106–15.)
19 *Ibid.*, p. 10.
20 Sunday O. Anozie, "Genetic Structuralism as a Critical Technique," *The Conch*, 3, No. 1 (1971), 33–44.
21 *Ibid.*, p. 42.
22 Sunday O. Anozie, *Sociologie du Roman Africain: Réalisme, Structure et Détermination dans le Roman moderne ouest-africain* (Paris, 1970). A portion of one chapter of this book has been translated into English and appears as "Structure and Utopia in Tutuola's *The Palm-Wine Drinkard*," *The Conch*, 2, No. 2 (1970), 80–88.
23 Sunday O. Anozie, *Christopher Okigbo: Creative Rhetoric* (London, 1972). A portion of one chapter of this book has been published as "A Structural Approach to Okigbo's *Distances*," *The Conch*, 1, No. 1 (1969), 19–29.

24 Sunday O. Anozie, "Structuralism in Poetry and Mythology (Towards a Study of African Vernacular and Oral Literature)," *The Conch*, 4, No. 1 (1972), 1–21.

ORAL TRADITION AND THE
INDIVIDUAL LITERARY TALENT

In his essay on "Tradition and the Individual Talent" T. S. Eliot comments on

> our tendency to insist, when we praise a poet, upon those aspects of his work in which he least resembles anyone else. In these aspects or parts of his work we pretend to find what is individual, what is the peculiar essence of the man. We dwell with satisfaction upon the poet's difference from his predecessors, especially his immediate predecessors; we endeavour to find something that can be isolated in order to be enjoyed. Whereas if we approach a poet without this prejudice we shall often find that not only the best, but the most individual parts of his work may be those in which the dead poets, his ancestors, assert their immortality most vigorously.[1]

Eliot's remark has a peculiar relevance to modern African literatures in English and French, even though these literatures do not have a long ancestry. Most of Africa's leading English- and French-writing poets, novelists and playwrights are not dead but alive and well and practicing their arts. To speak of African literary traditions, of lineal connections between one generation of writers and another, is almost impossible in literatures so young. African writers have barely developed identifiable chromosomes, much less transmitted their genes to posterity. It would be premature to expect an infant to produce recognizable offspring.

Yet the debate concerning what is original and what derivative in an individual author's work is an important one in African literary studies, and here T. S. Eliot is helpful. Though he speaks disparagingly of our tendency to be prejudiced in favor of idiosyncratic writers, he does not himself condemn individualism or originality in literary art. Novelty, he admits, is "better than repetition," far better than following the ways of one's predecessors in a "blind or timid adherence to [their] successes." The truly original writer is the one endowed with a "historical sense, . . . a perception, not only of the pastness of the past, but of its presence." He must be conscious of the living heritage of his culture and at the same time aware of his own place in it and relationship to it. It is "this historical sense, which is a sense of the timeless as well as of the temporal and of the timeless and of the temporal together, [that] makes a writer traditional."[2]

I have quoted Eliot at length because I believe his concept of the writer's "historical sense" is useful even when applied to a culture that lacks a long history of creative writing. If we substitute oral tradition for literary tradition, we remain in a good position to judge how "traditional" (in Eliot's sense of the word) a writer in a newly-literate culture may be and how effectively he makes use of the living heritage of the past to carve out a lasting place for himself in the present. We are in a position, in other words, to discriminate between writing that is original because it is a conscious, organic outgrowth from all that has existed before and writing that is derivative because it is an unthinking repetition of what has already been done. Indeed, if we pursue this line of reasoning far enough, we may ultimately be able to distinguish between literary works which are African in essence and those which are African only in their external trappings. But this may be carrying Eliotic ideas too far.

Let us admit at the outset that much African writing has been derivative. The earliest African authors were powerfully influenced by whatever literary models—oral or written—were available to them. The first lengthy prose narratives in Sesuto,[3] Yoruba[4] and Igbo[5] were transparent imitations of John Bunyan's *The Pilgrim's Progress*, which was usually among the first books after the Bible to be translated into an African vernacular language or used in a simplified English edition in missionary schools. Strong extra-literary incentives no doubt helped to lure the embryonic African muse into the straight and narrow paths of Bunyanesque allegory. The missionaries, who for many years held a virtual monopoly on both African education and vernacular publishing, needed moral reading matter as ammunition in their battles against illiteracy and paganism. Those authors whose manuscripts served evangelistic purposes were rewarded with quick publication (and possibly the promise of a higher reward later); others whose writings did not conform to the new morality stood little chance of seeing their works in print.[6] It is not surprising, then, that pioneers like Thomas Mofolo and D. O. Fagunwa began by emulating *The Pilgrim's Progress*, a text that was known to have earned the ecclesiastical stamp of approval.

After all, what else was there for them to emulate? They could not very well tamper with Holy Writ. If they started rewriting Bible stories so that Judas came out a hero, Jesus a psychopath with a martyr complex, and the hewers of wood and drawers of water a gang of discontented black workers who formed a labor union and refused to hew and draw, they knew they would very likely be raked over the coals for it. A writer could try his hand at simplifying Bible stories for school children, but he would have to remain faithful to his source. He could not distort or compromise the Word of God, and Heaven forbid that he should dare to add anything of his own invention! For writers with such limited possibilities, imaginative moral allegories patterned after *The Pilgrim's Progress* provided a creative outlet that was both safe and satisfying.

There was, of course, another direction in which they could move. They could record the oral lore of their people, suppressing the songs, sayings and stories that were off-color and singling out those that taught, or could be made to teach, an acceptable moral lesson. There was much greater interest in this kind of literary activity in the English colonies, where African vernacular languages were used as the medium of instruction in most elementary schools, than there was in the French territories, where the emphasis fell on the language and culture of "nos ancêtres les Gaulois." But some of the first African intellectuals to write creatively in the colonial tongues also produced literary redactions of oral tales. Cyprian Ekwensi's *Ikolo the Wrestler and Other Ibo Tales* (1947) and *An African Night's Entertainment* (a long Hausa tale recorded in 1947 but not published until 1962),[7] Birago Diop's *Les contes d'Amadou Koumba* (1947), and Léopold Senghor and Abdoulaye Sadji's *La belle histoire de Leuk-le-Lièvre* (1953) are examples of this genre of African writing. Like the vernacular authors who delved into folklore, these early *littérateurs* felt no compulsion to remain absolutely faithful to the oral tales they recounted. Their object was to tell an interesting story in an interesting way, partly to edify but mainly to entertain whoever might happen to read it. There was a degree of freedom, of creative play, in this kind of writing that was not possible in adaptations of Bible stories, but the final literary product was no less derivative. The only difference was that the raw material was taken from African rather than foreign sources.

There is still a good deal of derivative writing coming out of Africa today. Africans continue to publish collections of retold tribal tales and to mimic the literary fashions of Europe and America. It is the carbon copies of classic Western forms and techniques that are often most amusing to a Western reader, especially when they are crudely done and couched in diction that is either extremely dated or extremely contemporary. Aspiring African bards have composed solemn Horatian odes, romantic Petrarchan and Shakespearean sonnets, lofty Miltonic elegies, Pope-like heroic couplets, and Whitmanesque free verse; playwrights have experimented with drawing room comedy, epic tragedy, Brechtian expressionism, and theatre of the absurd; novelists have attempted to emulate such luminaries as Dickens, Hardy, Dumas, Faulkner, Joyce and Marie Corelli; and short story writers have enthusiastically responded to a wide variety of literary and cinematographic stimuli, ranging from Maupassant and O. Henry to true confessions, action-packed whodunits, sentimental melodramas and even Wild

West shoot'em-ups. Here is an example of verse that has been exhumed from a long-dead European poetic tradition. Written by someone appropriately named Erasmus Adeniyi, it was published in the Kano *Daily Comet*, a Northern Nigerian newspaper, in 1961, shortly after Patrice Lumumba's death.

SOONET TO PATRICE LUMUMBA

Cry now! lest thoughtless minds to aught avail
As Midas once did hail the carian home.
And yet Mobutu dares a thought to own
So far untutored by a first of mail.

Remember now! Ere Phoebe's rays do blind
Those very scions of Katanga's sway
With spectres sculptored from no mortal clay
Whose pallid mien and turgid eye assigned.

He strove, Lumumba strove, to stem the tide
Ere famine's famished maw protracted war
Relinguishing no dreg for Vulcan's bride.
Patrice the Dryads beckon to your law
Twixt Cape Town and the Lydian Hills
From Kenya's heights to sandy Ghanian shore. [8]

It seems a bit ironic that tribute to an African nationalist should be voiced in such an alien idiom. The poet does not seem to be aware that he himself has surrendered unconditionally to European cultural imperialism.

But not every African writer yielded so completely to foreign or indigenous literary influences. Some tried to combine the two traditions artistically, welding European form to African matter so skilfully that no one could tell without careful inspection precisely how or where they had been joined. These were the writers who began to contribute something new to world literature, for they were forging genuine links between the two disparate cultures Africans had inherited, one by birth, the other by education. Aimé Césaire and Léopold Senghor, in their negritude poetry, grafted African images and rhythms onto the surrealistic branch of French poetry. Camara Laye, in *Le regard du roi* (1954), transplanted Kafka to African soil and made him flourish there by pumping local sap into his expressionistic veins. The same kind of syncretism can be found today in a novel such as Yambo Ouologuem's *Le devoir de violence*, which appears to be an Islamicization of André Schwartz-Bart's *Le dernier des justes*.[9]

Several Western critics have argued that the early marriage of Europe and Africa in the poetry and fiction of French West Africa was no more legitimate or remarkable than the average shotgun wedding. Europe still took the active role, impregnating Africa with its creative force and thereby proving its superior cultural virility. Africa remained the passive partner, supinely accepting her master's gift until she began to notice her swelling creativity, whereupon she howled her anguish, blaming all her pains and troubles on colonial occupation of her virgin territory, yet still claiming the bastard offspring generated by this unwholesome union as her very own. Africa, according to these critics, had every right to slap a paternity suit on Europe, but she seemed to prefer to deny the liaison implicitly by stressing the social and spiritual differences that kept the cohabitants apart. In this colonial squabble, as in so many others, Europe was regarded as Reason, Africa Emotion.

Recent scholarship, however, affirms that Africa, even while assimilating Europe, never completely relinquished her own traditions, her own philosophy, her own principles of creative art. Janheinz Jahn outlines the history of African literature in European languages as follows:

> The writers at first may follow European models and find their strength in debate. But from one work to the next most of them take on more and more of African tradition, especially in recent years since the poetry of "Negritude" has lifted the ban and made the tradition respectable once more. This finally leads to the complete acceptance of African tradition, first among the lyric poets, and then also in the great story-tellers, until finally the European elements are simply assimilated as necessary materials into neo-African poetry and prose.[10]

The assimilation of foreign materials may have been a normal

African artistic impulse, for as Jahn points out in an essay on "Value Concepts in Sub-Saharan Africa":

> In African thinking, the universe consists of a network of living forces. . . . The universe is a unity in which each part depends on the others, and no part is changeless. If you take possession of a part of a thing, you thereby participate in its life force. . . . In NTU, the cosmic universal force, all single forces are tied together.[11]

So one could say that Césaire, Senghor, Laye and Ouologuem, by taking possession of European literary culture, participated in its life force, adding it to all the other life forces with which they were already familiar. Assimilation of things alien, absorption of new life forces, was itself an African esthetic principle. Thus Africa did not passively accept Europe's literature as foreign matter which would remain forever foreign, but creatively transformed it from something external into something internal. Africa, a cannibalistic culture, may have been forced to eat Europe raw, but it had no difficulty in completely digesting what it had consumed, in taking all the energy of the new life force into its own system.

One pungent example may suffice. Camara Laye's *Le regard du roi* is usually discussed as a regurgitation of modern German expressionism, as warmed-over Kafka. Wole Soyinka's comments on the novel are typical:

> . . . most intelligent readers like their Kafka straight, not geographically transposed. Even the character structure of Kafka's *Castle* has been most blatantly retained—Clarence for Mr. K.; Kafka's Barnabas the Messenger becomes the Beggar Intermediary; Arthur and Jeremiah, the unpredictable assistants, are turned into Nagoa and Noaga. We are not even spared the role of the landlord—or innkeeper—take your choice! It is truly amazing that foreign critics have contented themselves with merely dropping an occasional "Kafkaesque"—a feeble sop to integrity—since they cannot altogether ignore the more obvious imitativeness of Camara Laye's technique. (I think we can tell when the line of mere "influence" had been crossed.) Even within the primeval pit of collective allegory-consciousness, it is self-delusive to imagine that the Progresses of these black and white pilgrims have sprung

from independent creative stresses . . . the contemporary interpreters of African themes have not truly assimilated the new
idioms. It is merely naive to transpose the castle to the hut.[12]

This is the Europe-dominant, Africa-recessive theory of African
literary genealogy plainly stated. Laye's ancestors are traced to
Germany, not to Gaul or Guinea.

Soyinka's broadside attack on Laye recently provoked a firm
rebuttal from another Nigerian, J. M. Ita, a lecturer in the
Department of Modern Languages at the University of Ife. Ita
admits that there are many parallels between Kafka's *Castle* and
Le regard du roi, but he questions Soyinka's assumption that
"originality or creativeness necessarily lies in the treatment of
totally new material, as distinct from a fresh treatment of, or a
new approach to already existing material."[13] Ita goes on to
argue that

> in discussing the relationship of Laye's work to Kafka's, what we
> need to examine is not *whether* Laye has used Kafka's novels but
> *how* he has used them. Is he developing a theme present in Kafka's
> work, and remoulding what he borrows from the *Castle* so as to
> give it a new significance? If so, Laye's work constitutes a creative
> response—a reply, if one likes, to Kafka's. On the other hand if, in
> *The Radiance of the King*, Laye has merely reproduced chunks of
> Kafka haphazardly transposed into an African setting, then
> Soyinka is right to condemn the work as derivative.[14]

After a close and careful examination of the similarities and
differences between the two books and between the metaphysical assumptions of their authors (as revealed in their
books), Ita concludes:

> It is clear that Laye's novel is not a mere imitation of Kafka's, but
> is what I have called a "reply" to it. . . . In his novel, Laye has
> embodied a world which is not only different from Kafka's world,
> but is almost diametrically opposed to it, and in using Kafkan ele-
> ments he has consistently remoulded and re-organized them in
> such a way as to express this opposite vision. . . . African cultural
> integrity is likely to be endangered not so much when an *active*
> response is made to a foreign work, but when such works are pas-
> sively and unthinkingly accepted without criticism, comment or

any attempt to "reply" to them. . . . Laye has not "been influenced" by Kafka in the sense of having fallen under the domination of his imagination. We need have no anxiety on this score. It is Laye, not Kafka, who has done the assimilating.[15]

Ita's argument neatly illustrates Jahn's thesis and brings us back to Eliot's conception of the artist as incapable of true originality except in relation to the works of others. It is not *whether* the artist borrows but *how he uses* what he borrows that is crucially important. Furthermore, it doesn't really matter *who* or *where* he borrows from so long as his response is a genuinely creative one, so long as he "replies" in his own way to any stimulation he receives. Camara Laye responded creatively to Kafka's *Castle* by producing an indelibly African work of art in a European language and European literary form. This achievement proved him a highly original writer, not a slavishly derivative one. It also proved him an African artist who had mastered European tools, not a European artist who happened to be African. Any other African writer who succeeded in Africanizing a foreign source of inspiration—be it European, American or Asian—as well as a foreign literary language by completely assimilating them and using them to express his own vision of the human condition could lay claim to the same impressive creative accomplishment, the same artistic originality.

But what about those writers who turn to indigenous sources of inspiration, who try to exploit their own cultural heritage by making use of folktales, myths, proverbs, riddles, songs and other forms of African oral art in their literary works? Can their originality, their Africanness, be measured by the same yardstick? My answer is an emphatic yes. They not only *can*, they *must* be measured in precisely the same way with precisely the same instruments. An African novelist who makes use of the tar baby tale is not necessarily being more original or more "African" than another who builds his novel around the Cinderella story.[16] Everything will depend on *how* the material is used and *how well* it is integrated into his fiction.

The second criterion is probably more important than the

first. In a successful work of art, little or nothing will be wasted. Every character, every event, every detail will have some function, some reason for being what and where it is. If an artist clutters his canvas with distracting dabs of color which are non-functional or only minimally functional, his art will suffer. Likewise, the novelist, dramatist or poet who dabbles in folklore for no good reason risks losing far more than he could possibly gain by messing with it. Folklore, like any other ingredient in a work of literary art, must have an important role to have any significant value.

Let me attempt to illustrate this with reference to Nigerian literature in English, a literature remarkably rich in oral lore. Some Nigerian authors have been spectacularly successful in remolding oral art into literary art; others have been miserable failures. The degree of success or failure has often depended upon the author's resourcefulness in exploiting new esthetic opportunities afforded by the presence of one art form within another. Those who have taken advantage of the orality of the lore while remaining obedient to the discipline of their chosen literary medium have achieved a meaningful synthesis of two different modes of artistic expression. Others who have favored one mode at the expense of the other have been far less original in their manipulation of both. The most creative Nigerian writers have been those who have united the oral and literary "traditions" available to them.

Let us look at a few examples. To begin at the very beginning, the point at which Nigerian English literature itself began, there is Amos Tutuola, whose first book, *The Palm-Wine Drinkard and His Dead Palm-Wine Tapster in the Deads' Town*, aroused so much controversy when it was published twenty years ago.[17] English and American critics loved this strange story, partly because it was so delightfully odd and unexpected, partly because it was just what they would have expected to emerge from Africa—an uncouth, barbarous monster of a tale which had all the vitality and naiveté of childish illiterature. They praised Tutuola as a primitive genius with a mind and imagination of his own. Back home in Nigeria, however, the critical response was just the opposite. Educated Nigerians despised the book because it was not written in grammatical English and therefore did not reflect the level of learning and cultivation many of them had achieved. They also accused Tutuola of brazenly stealing his best material from Yoruba folktales and the Yoruba novels of D. O. Fagunwa. As far as they were concerned, he was not a creative writer but a plagiarist.

Notice that even in this early critical debate one of the key issues was the author's originality. The European commentators praised Tutuola for being different while the Nigerians condemned him for being the same as other Yoruba storytellers. This issue has continued to bedevil Tutuolan criticism, leading scholars to search for a definitive answer to the riddle of how much Tutuola borrowed from Fagunwa and oral tradition and how much he invented. The fruits of such research are questionable since it is impossible to weigh with scientific precision the debts and contributions of a creative imagination. One would have to know the entire cultural inventory that Tutuola had in stock before one could discriminate between stolen and manufactured goods. Otherwise one can only make assumptions from insufficient evidence.

Here, for instance, are two versions of a tale Tutuola may have had in mind when creating the "beautiful 'complete' gentleman" in *The Palm-Wine Drinkard*. Both versions were published in English in 1929, more than twenty years before Tutuola began writing his book.[18]

A handsome stranger once came into a village and strolled about among the people in mysterious silence. All the maidens admired him and wished that he would choose one of them for his bride. But he said nothing, and at last walked away into the forest and disappeared from sight.

A month later the stranger came again, and this time one of the maidens fell so much in love with him that she resolved to follow him into the forest, as she could not bear to be separated from him.

When the stranger looked back and saw her coming behind

him, he stopped, and begged her to return home; but she would not, and exclaimed: "I will never leave you, and wherever you go, I will follow."

"Beautiful maiden, you will regret it," replied the stranger sadly, as he hurried on.

After a while he stopped again, and once more begged her to retrace her steps; but she made the same reply, and again the handsome stranger said in sorrowful tones: "You will regret it, beautiful maiden!"

They went far into the depths of the forest, and at length reached a tree at the foot of which there lay a leopard-skin. Standing under the tree, the stranger began to sing a melancholy song, in which he told her that though he was allowed once a month to wander about in villages and towns like a man, he was in reality a savage leopard and would rend her in pieces as soon as he regained his natural form.

The second version is slightly longer and includes several additional motifs:

There is a certain country where the inhabitants have heads but no bodies. The Heads move about by jumping along the ground, but they never go very far.

One of the Heads desired to see the world, so he set out one morning secretly. When he had gone some distance, he saw an old woman looking out of the door of a hut, and he asked her if she would kindly lend him a body.

The old woman willingly lent him the body of her slave, and the Head thanked her and went on his way.

Later he came upon a young man sleeping under a tree, and asked him if he would kindly lend him a pair of arms, as he did not appear to be using them. The young man agreed, and the Head thanked him and went on his way.

Later still he reached a river-bank where fishermen sat singing and mending their cone-shaped net. The Head asked if any one of them would lend him a pair of legs, as they were all sitting and not walking. One of the fishermen agreed, and the Head thanked him and went on his way.

But now he had legs, arms, and a body, and so appeared like any other man.

In the evening he reached a town and saw maidens dancing while the onlookers threw coins to those they favoured. The Head threw all his coins to one of the dancers, and she so much admired his handsome form that she consented to marry him and go to live with him in his own country.

Next day they set out, but when they came to the river-bank, the stranger took off his legs and gave them back to the fisherman. Later they reached the young man who still lay sleeping under the tree, and to him the Head gave back his arms. Finally they came to the cottage, where the old woman stood watching, and here the stranger gave up his body.

When the bride saw that her husband was merely a Head, she was filled with horror, and ran away as fast as she could go.

In both of these tales an innocent maiden is lured away by a handsome stranger who turns out to be a disguised ogre. One can imagine such stories being told to impressionable young girls to warn them of what they might suffer if they were to allow themselves to be swept off their feet by attractive young men of whom they knew absolutely nothing. "Don't let handsome strangers lead you into the woods" is one of the more obvious morals that could be drawn from this kind of tale.

When Tutuola wove the story into *The Palm-Wine Drinkard*, he made the girl into a popular stereotype—the headstrong maiden who refuses all suitors.[19] The chance encounter in the marketplace between the girl and the "complete" gentleman is thus like a sudden collision between an irresistible force and a seemingly immovable object. The stubborn girl, overcome by the gentleman's extraordinary beauty, gives way completely, and then lives to regret her folly. But let's let Tutuola tell the story:

> . . . the daughter of the head of that town was a petty trader . . . her father was telling her to marry a man but she did not listen to her father; when her father saw that she did not care to marry anybody, he gave her to a man for himself, but this lady refused totally to marry that man who was introduced to her by her father. So that her father left her to herself.
>
> This lady was very beautiful as an angel but no man could convince her for marriage. So, one day she went to the market on a market-day as she was doing before, or to sell her articles as usual; on that market-day, she saw a curious creature in the market, but she did not know where the man came from and never knew him before.

[35]

THE DESCRIPTION OF THE CURIOUS CREATURE:—

He was a beautiful "complete" gentleman, he dressed with the finest and most costly clothes, all the parts of his body were completed, he was a tall man but stout. As this gentleman came to the market on that day, if he had been an article or animal for sale, he would be sold at least for £2000 (two thousand pounds). As this complete gentleman came to the market on that day, and at the same time that this lady saw him in the market, she did nothing more than to ask him where he was living, but this fine gentleman did not answer her or approach her at all. But when she noticed that the fine or complete gentleman did not listen to her, she left her articles and began to watch the movements of the complete gentleman about in the market and left her articles unsold.

By and by the market closed for that day then the whole people in the market were returning to their destinations etc., and the complete gentleman was returning to his own too, but as this lady was following him about in the market all the while, she saw him when he was returning to his destination as others did, then she was following him (complete gentleman) to an unknown place. But as she was following the complete gentleman along the road, he was telling her to go back or not to follow him, but the lady did not listen to what he was telling her, and when the complete gentleman had tired of telling her not to follow him or to go back to her town, he left her to follow him.

"DO NOT FOLLOW UNKNOWN MAN'S BEAUTY"

But when they had travelled about twelve miles away from that market, they left the road on which they were travelling and started to travel inside an endless forest in which only all the terrible creatures were living.

"RETURN THE PARTS OF BODY TO THE OWNERS; OR HIRED PARTS OF THE COMPLETE GENTLEMAN'S BODY TO BE RETURNED"

As they were travelling along in this endless forest then the complete gentleman in the market that the lady was following, began to return the hired parts of his body to the owners and he was paying them the rentage money. When he reached where he hired the left foot, he pulled it out, he gave it to the owner and paid him, and they kept going; when they reached the place where he hired

[36]

the right foot, he pulled it out and gave it to the owner and paid for the rentage. Now both feet had returned to the owners, so he began to crawl along on the ground, by that time, that lady wanted to go back to her town or her father, but the terrible and curious creature or the complete gentleman did not allow her to return or go back to her town or her father again and the complete gentleman said thus:—"I had told you not to follow me before we branched into this endless forest which belongs to only terrible and curious creatures, but when I became a half-bodied incomplete gentleman you wanted to go back, now that cannot be done, you have failed. Even you have never seen anything yet, just follow me."

When they went furthermore, then they reached where he hired the belly, ribs, chest etc., then he pulled them out and gave them to the owner and paid for the rentage.

Now to this gentleman or terrible creature remained only the head and both arms with neck, by that time he could not crawl as before but only went jumping on as a bull-frog and now this lady was soon faint for this fearful creature whom she was following. But when the lady saw every part of this complete gentleman in the market was spared or hired and he was returning them to the owners, then she began to try all her efforts to return to her father's town, but she was not allowed by this fearful creature at all.

When they reached where he hired both arms, he pulled them out and gave them to the owner, he paid for them; and they were still going on in this endless forest, they reached the place where he hired the neck, he pulled it out and gave it to the owner and paid for it as well.

"A FULL-BODIED GENTLEMAN REDUCED TO HEAD"

Now this complete gentleman was reduced to head and when they reached where he hired the skin and flesh which covered the head, he returned them, and paid to the owner, now the complete gentleman in the market reduced to a "SKULL" and this lady remained with only "Skull." When the lady saw that she remained with only Skull, she began to say that her father had been telling her to marry a man, but she did not listen to or believe him. (pp. 17–21)

It is obvious that Tutuola's version of this story, only part of which has been reproduced here, is richer in detail and more elaborate in dramatic design than either of the traditional tales we have examined. It would be tempting to conclude that the author has improved upon his sources and manufactured a singular silk purse out of a communal sow's ear. But what evidence—aside from the published traditional texts—can we offer to support this conclusion? How can we be certain that the tale Tutuola heard was any different from the one he recorded in his book? Tutuola once said that he learned the story of the Palm-Wine Drinkard from an old man on a Yoruba palm plantation whom he visited regularly on Sunday afternoons.[20] Perhaps it is this old man who should be credited with all the "originality" in Tutuola's narrative.

Yet literary critics keep singing Tutuola's praises as if he, like the fabled Drinkard, had returned from the land of the ancestral dead with magical power to create riches out of cultural poverty. Harold Collins speaks of him "updating, Westernizing, [and] adapting" native folktales "for his own purposes" and contributing "a great deal of elaboration" in such episodes as the one involving the self-dismembering "complete gentleman."[21] Eldred Jones, fallaciously assuming that the Yoruba tale upon which this particular episode is based closely resembles a unique Krio version current in Sierra Leone, applauds Tutuola for inventing several striking details which, though absent from the Krio version, are quite common in published Yoruba texts of the tale.[22] Since there are at least four (and perhaps as many as seven) different Yoruba texts of this tale available for comparison,[23] it is conceivable that different researchers working from these texts alone would still come to different conclusions about Tutuola's borrowings and lendings. This clearly is treacherous ground for the searcher after truth. The moral, of course, is that hunting for sources in the netherworld of oral tradition may not be too helpful in assessing an African literary artist's creativity, especially when the sources are as plastic as folktales and the artist as unorthodox as Tutuola.

A critic is on much safer footing if he studies the ways in which tales are twisted and braided together to form a consecutive narrative in *The Palm-Wine Drinkard*. Tutuola's literary skill is often revealed most plainly in his knitting of strong old fibers into interesting new patterns which have a logic and vitality of their own. He knows how to merge isolated traditional motifs into huge corporate conglomerates which move along on their own momentum, violating conventional codes of literary law and order by their directionlessness and disregard for standard forms of poetic justice. Sometimes he blends several different elements; sometimes he merely conjoins them in an arbitrary concatenation. But in order to effect his amalgamations he must alter the shape and occasionally the nature of his primary materials to suit a larger purpose. Again, it is not *what* the literary artist borrows but *how he uses* what he borrows that really matters.

Take the story of the handsome self-dismantling stranger, for instance. This tale does not stand alone in *The Palm-Wine Drinkard*. It is fully integrated into the larger saga of the Drinkard's search for his dead palm-wine tapster and cleverly joined to several other traditional tales and motifs which form a distinct segment of the saga. The Drinkard undertakes the "impossible task" of retrieving the headstrong girl from the "complete gentleman" in order to gain vital information from the girl's father, who claims to know where his dead palm-wine tapster can be found. The girl is being held in captivity in the land of the Skulls where she is forced to sit on a bullfrog and wear on her neck a cowrie which strikes her dumb and makes a terrible noise if she tries to escape. The Drinkard inconspicuously follows the "complete gentleman" home by transforming himself into a lizard and later frees the girl by transforming her into a kitten which he puts into his pocket before changing himself into a sparrow and flying away. But though he gets the girl home safely, he cannot cut the noisy cowrie off her neck, and until that is done and she can speak again, her father refuses to give him the information he seeks. The Drinkard returns to the land of Skulls and eavesdrops on the "complete gentleman reduced to skull," who while babbling to himself, reveals how the girl can be released from the double spell he cast on her. The

Drinkard applies the prescribed remedy, the girl returns to normal, and her father is so overjoyed that he rewards the Drinkard by giving him fifty kegs of palm-wine and the girl as his bride. "This," the Drinkard concludes etiologically, "was how I got a wife." Thereafter he always has a companion on his adventures. So this one brief episode, which begins as a simple irresistible force/immovable object story and develops into a complex cycle of tales built on a sequence of impossible tasks, deceptive strategies, miraculous shape-shifting, magical spells and generous rewards, changes the entire structure of the rest of the narrative. The busy train of events takes many turns but eventually arrives at a predetermined point. This is literary art.

It could be argued, of course, that Tutuola's techniques are no different from those of the oral storyteller, that he is more *raconteur* than *littérateur* despite his preference for Gutenberg's medium. After all, large epics from little legends grow in much the same fashion as *The Palm-Wine Drinkard* must have grown from Yoruba folktales. This argument seems to make good sense, but we must never forget that Tutuola wrote rather than spoke his story, so he had ample opportunity to plot and revise his narrative strategy as he went along. If he realized he had taken a false step early in his story, he could go back and correct it before releasing the full text to his audience. He could thus exercise much more control over his art than could an oral storyteller caught up in the active performance of a tale. Nevertheless, Tutuola's greatest contribution to world literature may be his transcendent orality, his ability to translate the techniques and materials of oral art into literary art.[24]

Now let's look at a bad example—Onuora Nzekwu, whose literary efforts are chock-full of ethnographic data on the Ibo of Eastern Nigeria. It has been reported that his first novel, *Wand of Noble Wood* (1961),[25] was "actually conceived as a piece of anthropology" and later transformed into full-length fiction.[26] This is easy to believe when we come across passages such as the following:

Beside me sat a man who had come in the Obi's entourage from Ado. I knew he had taken the *ozo*-title because of the eagle feather stuck in his cap and the leathern fan on his lap. After sipping my gin I coughed, trying to attract his attention.

"Please," I began. "I do not know your titular greeting." I was not being rude. It was the custom to ask if you did not know. It was a saying among us that one who asked never missed the way.

"Akunne," he told me, with some pride, mindful of his traditional status.

Among us *ozo*-title was the equivalent of the sacrament of Holy Orders. It was the only passport to officiating at offerings to ancestral spirits. *Ozo* was also a form of insurance policy which was neither transferable (except by the Obi) nor inherited. It guaranteed for the initiate a share of the fees paid by anyone who was initiated into the society after him. It was an expensive title which cost well over seven hundred pounds.

The titular greeting, Akunne, which meant mother's wealth, revealed that my companion had been initiated into the *ozo* society by means of wealth accumulated by his mother.

"Akunne," I echoed respectfully, in greeting.

"My son," he said, "who is your father in Ado?" This was one I expected. Our elders never asked who one was. They might never really understand if you told them. They always asked to know one's parents. Ado was not a very large town and the area in which the bulk of the indigenous population was concentrated was less than two square miles. It was therefore probable that any elder would know one's father or mother, particularly if they had grown up in the town. (pp. 12–13)

The main problem here is that Nzekwu is addressing a European audience to whom he feels he owes an explanation of the customs and practices of his people. Whenever he introduces a new word or idea he prefaces it with a self-conscious tag line such as "It was the custom to ask . . ."; "Among us . . ."; "Our elders never . . . ." Even the one scrap of native oral lore is neatly embalmed: "It was a saying among us that one who asked never missed the way." Throughout the novel Nzekwu relies on similar formulaic introductions to alert the reader to the bite of old saws: "Our people have a saying . . ." (p. 63); "Remember the saying . . ." (p. 81); "It is now I realize the truth of the saying . . ." (p. 120); "As our people say . . ." (p. 160); "It was our fathers who said. . . ." (p. 190) It is significant that when Nzekwu has his characters use European sayings such as "Blood is thicker than water," (p. 72) "Love is not love which alters when it alteration finds," (p. 118) and "Hell hath no fury like a woman scorned," (p. 173) he does not bother with introductions. He is confident that his European readers will recognize their own cultural heritage.

Nzekwu's second novel, *Blade Among the Boys* (1962), was no better than his first. There were fewer passages of textbook ethnography but the self-consciousness, the awkwardness, the artificial dialogue and the clumsily contrived conflicts between old and new cultures were still there. Nzekwu handled Ibo proverbs with greater ease but he did not try to delve as deeply into traditional life as he had before. It was not until he wrote his third novel, *Highlife for Lizards* (1965),[27] that he succeeded in creating a vivid portrait of rural Ibo society, a portrait which captured the color and rhythm of village life by faithfully reproducing the proverb-rich language of African peasants. Here, for example, is the way a man at a meeting of clan elders accuses his neighbor of treachery:

"But you and your wife forgot something—a smooth tongue carries a snail across thorns. It was providence that sent the wind that blew aside the fowl's tail-feathers to expose its anus; else, how could I have suspected you were planning to snatch my land from me? Well, let me warn you right now in the presence of everybody. Take your hands off my property. If you don't, the knife will either cut through the yam or the yam will break it." (p. 77)

Nzekwu had finally learned to make functional use of folklore. He had Africanized his fiction by tribalizing his prose style.

He had also learned how to exploit larger units of traditional oral lore artistically by deploying them strategically in his narrative. *Highlife for Lizards* is the story of a man with two wives, one old and barren, the other young and unfaithful. There is a strong rivalry between the women, partly because the elder feels displaced by the younger, who produces the first child in the family, partly because the younger believes the elder is still her husband's favorite. The fortunes of these women change radically as time passes. The elder finally becomes pregnant, the younger is chased away when discovered with another man, and the elder then wins back her husband's full affection by bearing his first son. Virtue is rewarded, vice punished in this domestic drama.

Halfway through the novel, at a time when the elder's fortunes are at such an ebb that she has been sent away from home temporarily so her husband can secretly contract a common law marriage with the younger woman, who is already wed to a man in a neighboring village, Nzekwu has one of his players tell a folktale. The narrator is the younger wife's first husband, from whom she is about to run away to join our hero's household; we see her absconding as he is telling the tale to a group of young children. The tale itself concerns a king who hates one of his wives "so much that he built her a hut away from the palace, close to the rubbish heap at the edge of the forest." (p. 93) This exiled wife's only friend is a monkey whom she teaches to dance and with whom she kindly agrees to exchange buttocks so that he can win a dancing competition in the land of animals. The monkey is to return her buttocks by a certain day, but he has a bad fall on his way home from the dancing arena and therefore fails to turn up at the appointed time. Meanwhile the unpopular wife has been seen bathing by one of the other queens, who reports her physical deformity to the king. The king decrees "that a week thence his queens would go naked in the town square and whichever of them was found to be subhuman would be beheaded." (p. 96) The exiled wife is now in desperate need of her buttocks and she wanders about the forest at night forlornly singing a song begging the monkey to return them. Parrots pick up the song and relay the message to the dying monkey, who sends the buttocks back via a special courier, a wizened old monkey who sympathetically gives ear to her tale and then provides her with a bunch of hairy bananas which she is warned not to eat. She is to leave the bananas alone and let anyone who wants them take them. The queen who had informed on her happens by, steals the whole bunch and greedily eats one after another until she notices she has sprouted a long tail. Horrified, she tries to cut, then burn, the tail off, but nothing works. The storyteller is beginning to wind up his yarn when he is interrupted by neighbors who report that his wife has just run away to live with another man in another village.

This fireside tale is very cunningly placed in the novel at precisely that point at which the hero's elder wife bears a striking resemblance to the heroine of the tale. Exiled and alienated from her people, she possesses a physical abnormality which makes her the laughing stock of her rivals and an embarrassment to her husband, who wants to have nothing to do with her. Yet she carries on bravely, remaining faithful to her marriage vows and showing great kindness to those who befriend her. Eventually her physical abnormality disappears, and her chief rival is brought low because of deviousness and disgraceful conduct. (There may even be some Freudian significance in the final reversal of buttocks and the consuming of strange bananas that leads to it.) In the end virtue triumphs, vice is vanquished, and all the good, honest and upright people live happily ever after.

Nzekwu makes this tale function as a paradigm of his novel, as a story with the same theme, message and structural pattern as the larger narrative in which it is set. The blueprint of the entire book is mirrored in this anecdote, which is deliberately introduced at the nadir of the heroine's career. By recapitulating past action and foreshadowing future events in this symbolic form at this significant moment, Nzekwu comments ironically on the mutability of human fortunes. The folktale thus functions as a parable as well as a paradigm, for it elaborates the novel's larger moral concerns while duplicating in miniature its basic artistic design. Nzekwu had finally learned to create literary art out of oral art.

How did he learn to do this? What influences acted upon him to transform him so quickly from a fourth-rate fictionalizing ethnographer into a fairly sophisticated literary craftsman? The answer cannot be sought in oral tradition, for it is unlikely that he learned any more about the folklore of his people between 1962 and 1965 than he had known before. The major difference between his two early novels and *Highlife for Lizards* was that now he knew how to make artistic use of folk material in his fiction; he had learned techniques by which he could harness the creative energy of traditional verbal art and make it serve a valuable literary purpose. He was doing better work because he had mastered new tools.

But how original was his achievement? Did he invent or merely borrow these new tools? Amos Tutuola had preceded him, but Tutuola had worked in realms of fantasy which required different imaginative skills, different creative instruments. Cyprian Ekwensi, another early Nigerian novelist, had specialized in African urban life, so there was nothing that his books could have taught Nzekwu about rural esthetic expression. T. M. Aluko, a Yoruba satirist, had far too much to learn himself to be able to pass on anything of value to another writer. All the evidence seems to point to Chinua Achebe, who had rapidly earned a reputation as Nigeria's leading novelist.

Achebe's first novel, *Things Fall Apart* (1958),[28] was a landmark in African fiction, for it rendered a fuller account of African tribal life before European contact than any novel had ever done before. Achebe accomplished this by presenting African experience from an African point of view rather than from the detached perspective of a foreign observer or with the self-conscious, almost apologetic attitude of an insider laboriously explaining his culture to outsiders. Achebe's Africa was neither the heart of darkness nor an anthropological case study; it was a human world inhabited by beings that a reader of any race or nationality could identify with and understand. Achebe "civilized" his African world by domesticating the English language and making it carry the full weight of what he wanted to say. His characters spoke and were spoken of in proverbs, metaphors, images and symbols that expressed their African experience.[29] Here is the way Achebe describes his hero in the opening pages of *Things Fall Apart*:

[45]

If ever a man deserved his success, that man was Okonkwo. At an early age he had achieved fame as the greatest wrestler in all the land. That was not luck. At the most one could say that his *chi* or personal god was good. But the Ibo people have a proverb that when a man says yes his *chi* also says yes. Okonkwo said yes very strongly; so his *chi* agreed. And not only his *chi* but his clan too, because it judged a man by the work of his hands. (pp. 22–23)

And later, when Okonkwo rashly commits the sin of beating one of his wives during the sacred Week of Peace,

. . . people said he had no respect for the gods of his clan. His enemies said his good fortune had gone to his head. They called him the little bird *nza* who so far forgot himself after a heavy meal that he challenged his *chi*. (p. 26)

Notice how skilfully the image of Okonkwo as a wrestler, as one who dares to struggle against his fate, is developed here.[30] Notice too how smoothly Achebe introduces the concept of *chi* into his narrative. Compare this finesse with Nzekwu's clumsy handling of the same concept in *Wand of Noble Wood*:

"I am sure Daddy will gladly do it for my sake. But I will have to buy him a goat," she added.

'Why?" I asked.

"He is an Ndichie, and you should have known that tradition compels each of them to sacrifice a goat to his *chi* any time he travels out of town."

Chi, according to our traditional religious doctrines, was a genius, a spiritual double connected with every individual's personality. Every individual had a *chi*, a guardian angel, on whom his success or failure in life depended, for fortune was the result of the application of one's *chi* to God. But *chi* had power only over one's material life and matter. (pp. 138–39)

Nzekwu's account may contain more anthropological information than Achebe's but it contains far less art.

By the time he wrote *Highlife for Lizards* Nzekwu had enough creative confidence to abandon these tedious explanations of tribal beliefs and customs. Now he sometimes went to the opposite extreme and employed Ibo words without any elucidation whatsoever. The *chi* concept, for example, suddenly pops up for

[46]

the first time in this novel in a conversation between two young women:

> "Suitors came and Father turned them away. He never asked my opinion or I would have been married long before I was sixteen."
> "If your chi had taken a fancy to any of the suitors," remarked Afulenu, "your father could not have stood in your way." (p. 20)

Chi is not even italicized here, much less explained. Nzekwu, like Achebe, was beginning to address his fiction to his own people, who did not need translations or ethnographic footnotes.

Achebe has had a profound influence on many other Nigerian novelists too, particularly the young Ibos who began writing in the nineteen-sixties. Authors like Nkem Nwankwo, Chukwuemeka Ike, Elechi Amadi, Flora Nwapa, E. C. C. Uzodinma, John Munonye and Clement Agunwa have followed in his footsteps, making use of many of the themes and techniques he introduced into Nigerian fiction. Nowhere is his inspiration more evident than in the way proverbs, folktales and other bits of oral lore are woven into the fabric of their novels. Achebe taught these writers to speak in an idiom that was distinctively African because it reverberated with echoes of traditional oral art. He made them into ventriloquists of culture by showing them how to translate their own rich verbal heritage into a new grammar of self-expression.

Yet in spite of his achievements, one might still ask, How original was Achebe? After all, here he was writing in a conventional Western literary form and pilfering some of his best material from venerable indigenous sources. Granted he may have produced an interesting hybrid by grafting native buds onto a foreign stalk and teaching other grafters to do the same, but was he really creating anything new? Wasn't he actually working well within the established boundaries of two traditions, one European, the other African?

To answer this question we must fall back on T. S. Eliot's definition of what makes a writer "traditional"; it is his "historical sense . . . a perception, not only of the pastness of the past, but of its presence . . . a sense of the timeless as well as of the temporal and of the timeless and of the temporal together."[31] Eliot believes that

> no poet, no artist of any art, has his complete meaning alone. His significance, his appreciation is the appreciation of his relation to the dead poets and artists. You cannot value him alone; you must set him, for contrast and comparison, among the dead.[32]

If we set Achebe among his European and African ancestors, I think we can see that he—and perhaps he alone among Nigerian novelists—possesses the "historical sense" that Eliot feels distinguishes the mature and truly original creative artist. Achebe is a "traditional" writer because he knows what to do with the traditions he inherited. As Eliot says in another place, the artist

> is not likely to know what is to be done unless he lives in what is not merely the present, but the present moment of the past, unless he is conscious, not of what is dead, but of what is already living.[33]

Achebe, because he possesses this consciousness in a way that other inventive artists like Amos Tutuola and Wole Soyinka do not, is at once the most traditional and the most original of Nigerian authors, and probably the only one alive who will have established a living literary tradition in his own lifetime.

NOTES

1 T. S. Eliot, *The Sacred Wood*, 3rd ed. (London, 1932), p. 48.
2 *Ibid.*, p. 49.
3 Thomas Mofolo, *Moeti oa Bochabela* (Morija: Morija Sesuto Book Depot, 1907). Janheinz Jahn, in *A History of Neo-African Literature* (London, 1968), pp. 100–01, states that a Sesuto translation of *The Pilgrim's Progress* did not exist prior to the publication of Mofolo's book. However, it seems likely that Mofolo knew of

Bunyan's work through the missionaries he worked for or through one of the early Xhosa or Zulu translations.

4 D. O. Fagunwa, *Ogboju Ode Ninu Igbo Irunmale* (London, 1950). L. Murby, in an "Editor's Foreword" to this edition, compares Fagunwa's work to "that great cornerstone of the English novel, Bunyan's *The Pilgrim's Progress.*"

5 O. R. Dathorne, "Ibo Literature: the Novel as Allegory," *Africa Quarterly*, 7 (1968), 365–68.

6 There is the famous example of Thomas Mofolo's *Chaka* (Morija: Morija Sesuto Book Depot, 1925), the Sesuto masterpiece which remained unpublished for seventeen years because missionaries found it objectionable.

7 Cyprian Ekwensi, "Outlook for African Writers," *West African Review*, January 1950, p. 19.

8 Erasmus Adeniyi, "Soonet to Patrice Lumumba," Kano *Daily Comet*, March 3, 1961, p. 4. All errors in the text have been preserved.

9 See Eric Sellin, "The Blueprint for Ouologuem's *Le devoir de violence*," *Research in African Literatures*, 2, No. 2 (1971). Sellin feels Ouologuem's borrowings come close to plagiarism. For further evidence of Ouologuem's literary debts, see "Something *New* out of Africa?," *Times Literary Supplement*, May 5, 1972, p. 525.

10 Janheinz Jahn, *Muntu* (New York, 1961), p. 211.

11 Janheinz Jahn, "Value Concepts in Sub-Saharan Africa," *Cross-Cultural Understanding: Epistemology in Anthropology*, ed. F. S. C. Northrop and Helen H. Livingston (New York, 1964), p. 56.

12 Wole Soyinka, "From a Common Back Cloth: A Reassessment of the African Literary Image," *American Scholar*, 32 (1963), 387–88.

13 J. M. Ita, "Laye's *Radiance of the King* and Kafka's *Castle*," *Odu*, N.S. No. 4 (1970), p. 19.

14 *Ibid.*

15 *Ibid.*, pp. 40–42.

16 At the American Folklore Society meeting held in Bloomington, Indiana in November, 1968, William Bascom reported that variants of the Cinderella tale had been found in Africa.

17 For discussion of this controversy, see Gerald Moore, *Seven African Writers* (London, 1962), p. 49; Harold R. Collins, *Amos Tutuola* (New York, 1969), pp. 20–22; and my "Amos Tutuola and His Critics," *Abbia*, No. 22 (1969), pp. 109–18.

18 M. I. Ogumefu, *Yoruba Legends* (London, 1929), pp. 18–19, 38–40. Tutuola was nine years old when this book of tales was published.

19 See, e.g., Barbara K. and Warren S. Walker, *Nigerian Folk Tales* (New Brunswick, N.J., 1961), pp. 22–23. All quotations from Tutuola are taken from *The Palm-Wine Drinkard and His Dead Palm-Wine Tapster in the Deads' Town* (New York, 1953).

20 *Listener*, November 13, 1952, p. 819.

21 Collins, *Amos Tutuola*, pp. 54–55.

22 Eldred Jones, "Amos Tutuola—*The Palm-Wine Drinkard: Fourteen Years On*," *Bulletin of the Association for African Literature in English*, No. 4 (1966), pp. 25–27.

23 See footnote 32 in *Abbia*, No. 22 (1969), p. 118.

24 This is discussed at greater length in Emmanuel Obiechina, "Amos Tutuola and the Oral Tradition," *Présence Africaine*, No. 65 (1968), pp. 85–106, and my "Amos Tutuola's *The Palm-Wine Drinkard* and Oral Tradition," which follows.

25 Onuora Nzekwu, *Wand of Noble Wood* (London, 1961). All quotations are taken from this edition.

26 John Povey, "Canons of Criticism for Neo-African Literature," *Proceedings of a Conference on African Languages and Literatures Held at Northwestern University, April 28–30, 1966*, ed. Jack Berry, *et al.* (n.p., n.d.), p. 79. This was mentioned earlier by Gerald Moore in "English Words, African Lives," *Présence Africaine*, No. 54 (1965), pp. 94–95.

27 Onuora Nzekwu, *Highlife for Lizards* (London, 1965). All quotations are taken from this edition.

28 Chinua Achebe, *Things Fall Apart* (London, 1958). All quotations are taken from this edition.

29 For further discussion of Achebe's style, see Eldred Jones, "Language and Theme in *Things Fall Apart*," *Review of English Literature*, 5 (October 1964), 39–43 and my "The Palm-Oil with Which Achebe's Words Are Eaten," which is reprinted in this volume.

30 I discuss this image at length in the article cited above.

31 Eliot, *Sacred Wood*, p. 49.

32 *Ibid.*

33 *Ibid.*, p. 59.

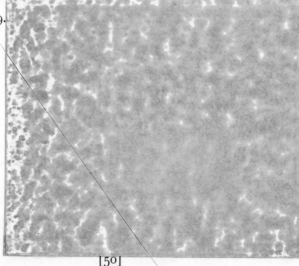

AMOS TUTUOLA'S
THE PALM-WINE DRINKARD AND
ORAL TRADITION

Amos Tutuola's *The Palm-Wine Drinkard* was the first substantial
literary work written in English by a Nigerian author, and its
publication in 1952 created a stir. Critics outside Nigeria were
enthusiastic, finding the story full of "weird and wonderful surprises" and the author's language "naive," "quaint" and
"amusing." Dylan Thomas called it a "brief, thronged, grisly
and bewitching story, written in young English," a "tall,
devilish story."[1] Underlying much of this criticism was the
notion that *The Palm-Wine Drinkard* was a highly original work
written by an untutored but extraordinarily imaginative native
genius.

In Nigeria the response of the critics was quite different.
Many educated Nigerians looked down upon Tutuola and fret-
ted that his imperfect control of English would come to be
regarded by the outside world as typical of Nigerian speech and
writing. Some tried to discredit *The Palm-Wine Drinkard* by
asserting that Tutuola had borrowed far more than he had
created. They cited Jungian archetypes, extended Yoruba folktales and the novels written in Yoruba by D. O. Fagunwa as
Tutuola's sources of inspiration.[2] In Nigerian criticism the
emphasis fell on Tutuola's lack of originality.

In 1958 the Nigerian view was given a boost by a well-
informed and dispassionate observer, Melville J. Herskovits,
who remarked in an introduction to a collection of Dahomean
tales that Tutuola was "drawing closely on the traditional
repertory of his culture"[3] in his first three books (*The Palm-Wine
Drinkard*, 1952; *My Life in the Bush of Ghosts*, 1954; *Simbi and the
Satyr of the Dark Jungle*, 1955). Without suggesting that these
works were any worse for such borrowing or that Tutuola

[51]

lacked creative literary talent, Herskovits went on to say, "It will be instructive for one who reads the narratives in this volume [*Dahomean Narrative*, 1958] to go to Tutuola's books with the motifs and orientations of the tales given here in mind. He will find them all."[4] Though this is certainly an overstatement, Herskovits's emphasis on Tutuola's debt to oral tradition lent impressive scholarly weight to the Nigerian critics' contention that *The Palm-Wine Drinkard* was not entirely original.

Even without Herskovits's testimony or any concrete proof of Tutuola's borrowings, the reader familiar with oral literature from Africa or elsewhere will find sufficient evidence in the text of *The Palm-Wine Drinkard* itself to convince him that Tutuola's writing has been greatly influenced by oral narrative art. The content, structure and style of the story bear the earmarks of oral tradition. To illustrate this, it is perhaps best to begin with a plot summary. One can do no better than again to quote Dylan Thomas, who in a book review entitled "Blithe Spirits," summarized *The Palm-Wine Drinkard* as a story

about the journey of an expert and devoted palm-wine drinkard through a nightmare of indescribable adventures, all simply and carefully described, in the spirit-bristling bush. From the age of ten he drank 225 kegs a day, and wished to do nothing else; he knew what was good for him, it was just what the witch-doctor ordered. But when his tapster fell from a tree and died, and as, naturally, he himself "did not satisfy with water as with palm-wine," he set out to search for the tapster in Deads' Town.

This was the devil—or, rather, the many devils—of a way off, and among these creatures, dubiously alive, whom he encountered, were an image with two long breasts with deep eyes; a female cream image; a quarter-of-a-mile-long total stranger with no head, feet or hands, but one large eye on his topmost; an unsoothing something with flood-light eyes, big as a hippopotamus but walking upright; animals cold as ice and hairy as sandpaper, who breathed very hot steam and sounded like church bells; and a "beautiful complete gentleman" who, as he went through the forest, returned the hired parts of his body to their owners, at the same time paying rentage, and soon became a full-bodied gentleman reduced to skull.

Luckily, the drinkard found a fine wife on his travels, and she

bore him a child from her thumb; but the child turned out to be
abnormal, a pyromaniac, a smasher to death of domestic animals,
and a bigger drinkard than its father, who was forced to burn it to
ashes. And out of the ashes appeared a half-bodied child, talking
with a "lower voice like a telephone." . . . There is, later, one
harmonious interlude in the Faithful-Mother's house, or magical,
techni-colour night-club, in a tree that takes photographs; and
one beautiful moment of rejoicing, when Drum, Song, and Dance,
three tree fellows, perform upon themselves, and the dead arise,
and the animals, snakes, and spirits of the bush dance together.
But mostly it's hard and haunted going until the drinkard and his
wife reach Deads' Town, meet the tapster, and, clutching his gift
of a miraculous, all-providing Egg, are hounded out of the town
by dead babies. . . .[5]

As can be seen from this summary, *The Palm-Wine Drinkard* is
pure fantasy, a voyage of the imagination into a never-never
land of magic, marvels and monsters. But the beings and the
doings in this fantasy world are not entirely unfamiliar to us.
The journey to the land of the dead, the abnormal conception,
the monstrous child, the enormous drinking capacity, the all-
providing magical object, the tree-spirits, the personifications,
the fabulous monsters—these are standard materials of oral
tradition, the stuff folktales are made of all over the world.

The palm-wine drinkard himself appears at first to be an
unpromising hero. He has, after all, done nothing but drink
palm-wine all his life. But once he gets started on his journey to
Deads' Town, his extraordinary cleverness and unusual powers
of endurance enable him to circumvent or survive numerous
misadventures. He carries with him a substantial supply of juju
so he can transform himself at will whenever he gets into a tight
corner. However, even though he is part-trickster, part-
magician, part-superman, he cannot overcome every adversary
or extricate himself from every difficult situation; supernatural
helpers have to come to his assistance from time to time. Eventually he finds his tapster in Deads' Town but cannot persuade
him to reenter the world of the "alives." The palm-wine drinkard
and his wife leave Deads' Town and, several adventures later,
arrive home only to discover that their people are starving.

Heaven and Land have had a bitter quarrel and Heaven has refused to send rain to Land. The ensuing drought and famine have killed millions. The palm-wine drinkard springs into action and in a short time manages to feed the remaining multitudes, settle the cosmic dispute, end the drought and famine, and restore the world to normal functioning order. The unpromising hero who had set out on his quest with limited powers and purely selfish ambitions becomes in the end a miracle worker, the savior and benefactor of all mankind. He changes, in other words, from a typical folktale hero to a typical epic hero. Such a change does not take him outside the stream of oral tradition.

Further evidence that *The Palm-Wine Drinkard* is largely derived from oral tradition can be found in the inner structure of the narrative. Some critics have overlooked this evidence because they have focused only on the frame or superstructure of the story. Gerald Moore, for example, praising Tutuola's "grasp of basic literary forms," described the palm-wine drinkard's deliberate quest for his dead palm-wine tapster, a quest in the course of which the drinkard experiences many trials, labors and revelations, as a "variant . . . of the cycle of the heroic monomyth, Departure—Initiation—Return."[6] This is a perceptive comment on the superstructure of the story, but a close examination of the inner structure, of the way in which individual episodes are constructed, set in sequence and woven together into a coherent design, suggests that Tutuola should be credited as much with a grasp of the basic forms of spoken art as with "a grasp of basic literary forms." Indeed, the fact that the story consists entirely of a series of short, separable episodes immediately arouses a suspicion that it is little more than a medley of traditional tales strung together on the lifeline of a common hero. This suspicion is strengthened when we find many of these episodes are rounded off with closing formulas. For example: "This was how I got a wife."[7] "That was how we got away from the long white creatures." (p. 43) "That was how we were saved from the Unknown creatures of the 'Unreturnable-Heaven's town.' " (p. 63) "This was the end of the story of the bag which I carried from the bush to the 'wrong town.' " (p. 95) Several episodes even have etiological endings; for example, "So that since the day that I had brought Death out from his house, he has no permanent place to dwell or stay, and we are hearing his name about in the world " (p. 16) Etiological tales and closing formulas are quite common in West African oral tradition.

The Palm-Wine Drinkard's neat cyclical superstructure rests on a very loosely coordinated inner structure. The hero is involved in one adventure after another, but these adventures are not well integrated. Like boxcars on a freight train, they are independent units coupled with a minimum of apparatus and set in a seemingly random and interchangeable order. There is no foreshadowing of events, no dramatic irony, no evidence of any kind that the sequence of events was carefully thought out. Tutuola appears to be improvising as he goes along and employing the techniques and materials of oral narrative art in his improvisations. To search for an orderly system or a well-developed artistic pattern in the chain of disjointed episodes in *The Palm-Wine Drinkard* is to search for symmetry in chaos, for deliberate design in chance. Some critics have risen to the challenge with bold imagination. Gerald Moore has found it

> of the utmost significance that the first of all the trials imposed upon [the palm-wine drinkard] in his journey is the binding and bringing of Death. . . . It stands as a clear enough indication that the Drinkard's adventure is not merely a journey into the eternal African Bush, but equally a journey into the racial imagination, into the sub-conscious, into that Spirit World that everywhere co-exists and even overlaps with the world of waking "reality."[8]

Unfortunately, this interesting creative interpretation is built on a factual error. The first of the trials imposed upon the palm-wine drinkard in his journey is not the binding and bringing of Death but rather the fetching of an unnamed object from an unnamed blacksmith in an unnamed town. An old man has promised to tell the drinkard where his tapster is if the drinkard can accomplish this impossible task. The drinkard succeeds in fetching the object, and the old man, instead of rewarding him, sets him a still more impossible task—the binding and bringing of Death. When the drinkard accomplishes this dreadful task, the old man and all the rest of the people in the town flee in terror.

The plot of this adventure resembles that found in many folk-tales. A hero must perform impossible tasks in order to gain important information. Each successive task is more difficult to perform. When the hero succeeds in performing the most diffi-cult task, usually a task in which he must risk his life, the task-setter, amazed and terrified, flees and never bothers the hero again. In such tales the function of the impossible tasks is to provide opportunities for an extraordinary hero to display his extraordinary abilities. But neither the tasks nor the hero's special skills in coping with them need figure in the tale again. Each successful performance of an impossible task can stand as a complete and independent tale within the main tale, an event which need not be closely related to previous or subsequent events.

And such is the case in the episode of the binding and bringing of Death. Nothing in this episode carries over into other epi-sodes. The drinkard's triumph over Death is not permanent; he soon faces threats on his life again. What is most significant about this first contest with Death is not its place in the super-structure of the story but its place in one segment of the inner structure; not, in other words, the fact that it launches the reader on a journey into the eternal African bush, the racial imagination, the subconscious or the African Spirit World, but the fact that it has the form, place, and function of an enclosed motif in an extended folktale. This episode affords structural evidence of Tutuola's debt to oral tradition.

The style of *The Palm-Wine Drinkard* is essentially an oral style. The story is told by the drinkard himself, and right from the beginning we sense that he is speaking, not writing, of his experiences. Here are his first words:

> I was a palm-wine drinkard since I was a boy of ten years of age. I had no other work more than to drink palm-wine in my life. In

those days we did not know other money, except COWRIES, so that everything was very cheap, and my father was the richest man in our town.

My father got eight children and I was the eldest among them, all of the rest were hard workers, but I myself was an expert palm-wine drinkard. I was drinking palm-wine from morning till night and from night till morning. By that time I could not drink ordinary water at all except palm-wine.

But when my father noticed that I could not do any work more than to drink, he engaged an expert palm-wine tapster for me; he had no other work more than to tap palm-wine every day.

So my father gave me a palm-tree farm which was nine miles square and it contained 560,000 palm-trees, and this palm-wine tapster was tapping one hundred and fifty kegs of palm-wine every morning, but before 2 o'clock p.m., I would have drunk all of it; after that he would go and tap another 75 kegs in the evening which I would be drinking till morning. So my friends were uncountable by that time and they were drinking palm-wine with me from morning till a late hour in the night. (p. 7)

The entire story is told in this naive tall-tale style, an idiom which preserves the flavor and rhythm of speech. Mabel Jolaoso, a Yoruba reviewer of Tutuola's books, notes that the "loose structure of his sentences, his roundabout expressions, and his vivid similes, essentially African, remind one very forcibly of the rambling old grandmother telling her tale of spirits in the ghostly light of the moon."[9] Tutuola did not have to work to create this style; it was perfectly natural to him. A *West Africa* interviewer reported in 1954 that his "spoken and written English are identical and he writes exactly what presents itself to his mind."[10] Another Yoruba critic confirmed this, adding only that Tutuola's writing "consists largely in translating Yoruba ideas into English."[11] According to anthropologist Paul Bohannan, many felt that *The Palm-Wine Drinkard* was "the same sort of thing that any Lagos Yoruba could talk."[12] It was merely oral art written down.

The influence of Tutuola's native language on his prose style can be seen in the passage quoted above. Unorthodox constructions such as "I had no other work more than to drink," "I could not do any work more than to drink," "he had no other work more than to tap," and "we did not know other money, except COWRIES" are taken directly from Yoruba (mo owó mǐràn, àfí ẹya owó). The phrase "by that time" (n'ígbà yẹn) is also used in typical Yoruba fashion.[13] It may have been stylistic eccentricities like these that led Mabel Jolaoso to remark that "the very imperfections of Tutuola's English have made him the perfect African storyteller."[14] In syntax as well as imagery and narrative content he sounded exactly like a Yoruba raconteur.

Of course, one may argue that oral narratives are not usually told in the first person and that Tutuola's narrative technique in *The Palm-Wine Drinkard* is therefore uncharacteristic of oral tradition. Unless we wish to try to counter this argument by pretending that Tutuola is a Nigerian Münchhausen, we must admit that the drinkard-narrator is a persona, a literary convenience. Paradoxically, it is by using a persona that Tutuola manages to achieve and sustain an oral style in *The Palm-Wine Drinkard*, and oral style plays a crucial role in unifying the story. Only when we hear the same authentic human voice speaking to us in every episode are we willing to suspend our disbelief in the incredible chain of incongruous events unraveling before us. Tutuola, by using the drinkard as a persona, creates a coherent work of art which bridges literary tradition and oral tradition.

Tutuola is the sort of artist who can blend two traditions without feeling uncomfortable. Whatever he borrows or adapts soon becomes his own. His fertile imagination, never fettered by logic or common sense, begets the incongruous, the unorthodox, the unexpected, the bizarre. Some of his most original creations are the splendidly grotesque monsters in *The Palm-Wine Drinkard*. Here, for example, is his description of a man-eating "red fish":

. . . its head was just like a tortoise's head, but it was as big as an elephant's head and it had over 30 horns and large eyes which surrounded the head. All these horns were spread out as an umbrella. It could not walk but was only gliding on the ground like a snake and its body was just like a bat's body and covered with long red hair like strings. It could only fly to a short distance, and if it shouted a person who was four miles away would hear. All the eyes which surrounded its head were closing and opening at the same time as if a man was pressing a switch on and off. (pp. 79–80)

The umbrella-like horns and the electrically operated eyes are arresting images. Tutuola frequently surprises his readers with such comparisons. An angry king has "hot steam . . . rushing out of his mouth as a big boiler." Rolling skulls sound like "a thousand petrol drums . . . pushing along a hard road." Many other contrivances of modern civilization—bombs, razor blades, cigarettes, sandpaper, telephones, floodlights, football fields— are scattered in similes throughout the narrative. No doubt Tutuola saw nothing odd or inappropriate about including modern civilization in the palm-wine drinkard's world of experience.

The evidence presented here strongly suggests that *The Palm-Wine Drinkard* has been greatly influenced by oral tradition. The hero appears to be a composite of the heroes found most frequently in African oral narratives—the trickster, the magician, the superman, the unpromising hero, the culture hero—and he tells his story in an oral style. The story itself is little more than a cleverly woven string of loosely connected episodes, many of which appear to have been borrowed or derived from folktales and embellished with details from the technology of modern civilization. By keeping one foot in the old world and one in the new while translating oral art into literary art, Tutuola bridges two traditions. Herein lies his originality.

NOTES
1 Dylan Thomas, "Blithe Spirits," *The Observer*, July 6, 1952, p. 7.
2 For discussion of the Nigerian reaction, see Gerald Moore, *Seven African Writers* (London, 1962), p. 49; Harold R. Collins,

"Founding a New National Literature: The Ghost Novels of Amos Tutuola," *Critique*, 4 (1960–61), 17–28, or *Amos Tutuola* (New York, 1969), pp. 20–22, 87–95; and my "Amos Tutuola and His Critics," *Abbia*, No. 22 (1969), pp. 109–18. Further discussion of Tutuola can be found in Eldred D. Jones, "Amos Tutuola—*The Palm-Wine Drinkard:* Fourteen Years On," *Bulletin of the Association for African Literature in English*, No. 4 (March 1966), pp. 24–30, and E. N. Obiechina, "Transition from Oral to Literary Tradition," *Présence Africaine*, No. 63 (1967), pp. 146–47.

3 Melville J. Herskovits and Frances S. Herskovits, *Dahomean Narrative. A Cross-Cultural Analysis* (Evanston, 1958), p. 13.

4 *Ibid.*

5 Thomas, "Blithe Spirits," p. 7.

6 Moore, *Seven African Writers*, p. 44. Here Moore cites Joseph Campbell's *The Hero With a Thousand Faces* (1949), a study of the monomyth.

7 Amos Tutuola, *The Palm-Wine Drinkard and His Dead Palm-Wine Tapster in the Deads' Town* (New York, 1953), p. 31. All quotations are taken from this Grove Press edition.

8 Moore, pp. 44–46.

9 Mabel Jolaoso, a review in *Odu*, No. 1 (January 1955), p. 43.

10 *West Africa*, May 1, 1954, p. 389.

11 Babasola Johnson, "The Books of Amos Tutuola," *West Africa*, April 10, 1954, p. 322.

12 Paul Bohannan, "Translation—A Problem in Anthropology," *Listener*, May 13, 1954, p. 815.

13 I wish to thank Edward Fresco, formerly a doctoral candidate in linguistics at the University of California at Los Angeles, for helping me to locate the Yoruba elements in this passage.

14 Jolaoso, p. 43.

AMOS TUTUOLA'S
TELEVISION-HANDED GHOSTESS

Amos Tutuola, the Nigerian coppersmith who blundered his way through the English language to become one of Africa's best known authors, is still regarded by most critics of African writing as a literary freak.[1] His lack of schooling, his eccentric handling of grammar and syntax, his preoccupation with fantasy and fable, and his bizarre, almost surrealistic imagination are usually singled out as reasons for excluding him from serious consideration when discussing the development of the African novel or, more broadly, the evolution of English-language literature among peoples who do not have English as their native tongue. Tutuola, it is argued, is not a typical African writer; he must be viewed as the exception rather than the rule—the black sheep, so to speak, in the African literary family. Moreover, he has shown no capacity for creative development, no desire to join the mainstream. His unkindest critics, denying he has written six books, insist that he has merely written one book six times, using the same mythic quest pattern (Departure—Initiation—Return) in each. He has been branded a literary cul-de-sac, a fantastic primitive, a myopic visionary, a lucky accident—everything, in fact, but what he really is, the most African of African writers.

No one, of course, would seriously attempt to dispute the fact that he has been greatly influenced by African oral tradition.[2] Indeed, this is often held up as further proof of his freakishness as a writer. "Who but Tutuola," critics hoot, "would appropriate a European language, borrow a European literary form, steal much of his imagery from European technology and yet remain uncompromisingly aboriginal in his method of story-telling?" To some this kind of eclecticism is evidence of unsophisticated syncretism, a naive blending of two separate and culturally distinct modes of narrative. Tutuola is considered odd because in marrying Europe to Africa, he allows Africa to stand as the senior partner. He does not surrender unconditionally to European culture. Unlike his better educated compatriots who write realistic novels in the manner of Hardy or Hemingway and poetry echoing Eliot, Pound and Hopkins—voices which any well-bred Westerner can recognize—Tutuola seems immune to specific foreign literary influences. A few critics, desperate for familiar touchstones, have attempted to compare him to great fabulists such as Dante, Blake and Bunyan,[3] but the lines of comparison always have to be drawn oblique rather than parallel. For Tutuola, though obviously Westernized, is not a Western writer; he is *sui generis*, a rare aberration separated from the rest of literary mankind by his stubborn Africanness, his unremitting orality. Or so, at least, it seems to most of his critics, who cannot find a convenient pigeonhole in which to place him.

The truth of the matter is that Tutuola's *africanité* owes as much to African literary sources as to African folklore. He has borrowed extensively not only from Yoruba folktales but also from the Yoruba "novels" of the late Chief Daniel O. Fagunwa,[4] the most prolific vernacular writer in Western Nigeria. Furthermore, even when Tutuola appears to be stepping outside his own culture to make use of foreign materials, he may in fact be operating entirely within a Yoruba esthetic framework. His images and props may be European, but his exploitation of them will be characteristically African.[5] To demonstrate just how parochial this universal writer is, I propose to turn to his second book, *My Life in the Bush of Ghosts*,[6] and examine his hero's famous encounter with the "Television-handed Ghostess."

Before meeting this unearthly creature, the narrator-hero has had numerous harrowing adventures. Separated at age seven from his mother and brother during a slave raid, he had accidentally stumbled into the Bush of Ghosts while seeking refuge in a hole in the ground and had spent the next twenty-four years trying to find his way out. Wandering from town to town in this

African spirit world, he had been captured by the malodorous
king of the Smelling Ghosts, had escaped by magically transforming himself into a cow (only to be chased by a lion and
captured by ghostly cowboys), had later learned ghost language
and married the sister of a young Burglar Ghost, had also married a "Super Lady" who bore him a monstrous half-human,
half-ghostly son, and had endured various ordeals, such as being
encased in a pitcher, wrapped up chrysalis-fashion in spider
webs, buried alive in a coffin, arrested by mosquito-worshipping
ghosts and sentenced without trial to sixteen years at hard labor
in an oven which he himself had to stoke. Amidst these tribu-
lations he had occasionally had a few pleasant experiences, such
as meeting his dead cousin who was working as a Christian
missionary in the 10th Town of Ghosts, a well-regulated urban
center replete with schools, hospitals, police stations, law courts,
prisons, even a Methodist church; the hero had remained in this
pleasant setting for several years, first taking a six-month course
so he could qualify as a "full dead man." But eventually he
resumes his journey and now comes face to face with one of the
most hideous of all ghosts:

> She was not more than three feet high. Immediately she entered
> [the hut] she went direct to the fire, she spread the mat closely to
> the fire and then sat down on it without saluting or talking to me.
> So at this stage I noticed carefully that she was almost covered
> with sores, even there was no single hair on her head, except sores
> with uncountable maggots which were dashing here and there on
> her body. Both her arms were not more than one and an half foot,
> it had uncountable short fingers. She was crying bitterly and re-
> peatedly as if somebody was stabbing her with knives. . . . When I
> could not bear her cry I asked her—"by the way what are you cry-
> ing for?" She replied—"I am crying because of you." Then I
> asked again—"because of me?" She said—"yes" and I said—
> "What for?" Then she started to relate her story thus—
>
> "I was born over two hundred years ago with sores on my head
> and all over my body. Since the day that I was born I have no
> other work more than to find out the doctor who could heal it for
> me and several of them had tried all their best but failed. Instead
> of healing or curing it would be spreading wider and then giving

[63]

me more pains. I have been to many sorcerers to know whether the sore would be healed, but every one of them was telling me that there is an earthly person who had been lost in this Bush of Ghosts, so that if I can be wandering about I might see you one day, and the sorcerers said that if you will be licking the sore every day with your tongue for ten years it would be healed. So that I am very lucky and very glad that I meet you here today and I shall also be exceedingly glad if you will be licking the sore with your tongue every day until the ten years that it will be healed as . the sorcerers had told me." (pp. 161–62)

She goes on to claim that she is crying because of the many hardships he has had to endure in the Bush of Ghosts, and then, to induce him to endure one more, she hints that she knows how he can get home. Our hero, unmoved, replies:

"I want you to go back to your sorcerers and tell them I refuse to lick the sore." After I told her like this she said again—"It is not a matter of going back to the sorcerers, but if you can do it look at my palm or hand." But when she told me to look at her palm and opened it nearly to touch my face, it was exactly as a television, I saw my town, mother, brother and all my playmates, then she was asking me frequently—"do you agree to be licking the sore with your tongue, tell me, now, yes or no?" (p. 163)

The hero is in a true quandary:

I thought over how the sore was dirty and smelling badly, especially those maggots which were dashing here and there all over the sore, so it was hard for me to say "yes." But as I was seeing my town with all my people, it was also hard for me to say "No." (p. 164)

Luckily, while the hero is watching a second showing of this supernatural Candid Camera, he sees his earthly mother prepare a native remedy to heal a sore on a baby's foot. The hero tries the same prescription on the ghostess and within a week she is cured. The television-handed ghostess then lives up to her part of the bargain:

. . . she opened her palm as usual, she told me to look at it, but to my surprise, I simply found myself under the fruit tree which is near my home town. . . . It was under this fruit tree my brother

[64]

left me on the road when he was running away from the enemies' guns which were driving me farther and farther until I entered into the Bush of Ghosts, and it was the fruit of this tree I ate first immediately I entered the Bush of Ghosts. This is how I got out of the Bush of Ghosts, which I entered when I was seven years old. (p. 166)

The comparisons linking Tutuola to Dante, Blake and Bunyan may now appear to have some validity, but it can be demonstrated that Tutuola is actually much closer to his fellow tribesman, Chief Fagunwa, than to any other writer. Fagunwa, who wrote in Yoruba, published at least nine books between 1948 and 1951,[7] the years immediately preceding the publication of Tutuola's first two works,[8] and there can be no doubt that Tutuola learned a lot from Fagunwa's writings. Tutuola himself has more or less admitted to this,[9] but even without such an admission the debt would be obvious to anyone reading their books. Here, for example, is Fagunwa's description of a repulsive creature one of his heroes meets on an expedition to Mount Langbodo, which lies on the other side of the Forest of a Thousand Daemons, near the dome of Heaven:[10]

One morning, as we made our way along, I caught sight of a man who went by the name of Egbin. In fact we began to smell him even before we set eyes on him. My good friends, since the day I was born into this world I have never encountered such a disgusting object as this man. All his toes were pocked with the jigger and they were so numerous that they had cut through several of his toes and infested his legs from the soles to the knees and many of them even came out of their own accord as he walked. The sores on his legs were numerous and he covered them with broad leaves, for the smallest of them was at least the size of my palm, many of them were left uncovered because these leaves could not fully cope with their size and they oozed fluids and pus as he moved. Egbin never cleaned his anus when he excreted and crusts of excrement from some three years back could be found at the entrance to his anus; when he rested, worms and piles emerged from his anus and sauntered all over his body, and he would pull them off with his hands; when he wanted to excrete he never stopped in one spot, he voided as he walked and the faeces stuck to his thighs and stuck to his legs. Every kind of boil and tumour lined the body of this man and each one was bigger than my foot, they burst open on his body and he would gather the suppuration in his hand and lick it up. Egbin never bathed, it was taboo. The oozing from his eyes was like the vomit of a man who has eaten corn porridge, he stank worse than rotten meat and maggots filled his flesh. His hair was as the skin of a toad, grime from eternities was plastered on it, black he was as soap from palm oil. Earthworms, snakes, scorpions and every manner of crawly creatures came out from his mouth when he spoke and he would chew on them whenever he was hungry. The mucus never dried in Egbin's nostrils, this he used as water for cooking his food and he drank it also as water. (p. 94)

Although this delicious portrait is not a mirror image of Tutuola's television-handed ghostess, the two characters have enough in common to reflect a lineal relationship. They are kissing cousins, if nothing else. But probably they are much more akin, Fagunwa's Egbin having presumably sired Tutuola's ghostess. Both creatures are virtually hairless and pocked with oozing sores which require extensively licking.[11] Each supports an army of active parasites; the ghostess has "uncountable maggots . . . dashing here and there on her body," while Egbin has not only maggots but anal worms and piles sauntering all over his. Egbin smells much worse than the ghostess, but this is probably due to the fact that Tutuola had practically exhausted his olfactory imagery on the king of the Smelling Ghosts, who, like Egbin, had an insect-infested body "full of excreta, urine and also wet with the rotten blood of all the animals that he was killing for his food." (p. 29)

More important than these matching visual and nasal details, however, is the similarity in the rhetorical structure of such descriptions. Both Fagunwa and Tutuola pile up details, repeating the same idea over and over again through variations in imagery. They are not content with economical descriptions of how badly Egbin smells or how painfully the ghostess oozes; they must enlarge upon the notion, embroider it, play with it, elaborating it in so many different ways that we cannot avoid carrying away a vivid impression of the enormity of the abnormality. I have argued elsewhere[12] that in expressing themselves

[66]

in this kind of ebullient style, both authors may be exploiting a traditional mode of Yoruba humor, a mode that relies upon inventive comic exaggeration and verbal extravagance. Such rhetoric is not found only in literary works. Tutuola and Fagunwa may owe a great deal of their stylistic brilliance to Yoruba oral tradition.

Certainly both writers are more in debt to the African fireside raconteur than to the European man of letters. This is evident in content and narrative structure as well as style. The motifs and organization we find in Tutuola's television-handed ghostess episode appear to derive almost exclusively from indigenous sources. The ghost world is an African ghost world, for as Gerald Moore has pointed out,

> the ghosts . . . are not the individual spirits of those who once lived on earth; they are the permanent inhabitants of the Otherworld, who have never lived as mortals, but who have intimate knowledge of that life and are in constant intercourse with it. At the same time, it appears that earthly witches and wizards hold their meetings among these ghosts and that it is from there that "spirit-children" are sent to dwell among men and act as agents for the ghost world.[13]

Moore goes on to say that "none of this is worked out with theological exactitude," and indeed, we do encounter a few stray mortal ghosts such as the dead cousin in the 10th Town of Ghosts, but the distinctively African character of this spirit world is indisputable. Furthermore, Alice Werner, in her study of African mythology, notes that among many tribes the ghost world is usually reached "through caves or holes in the earth," and that stories of human beings who have penetrated into this subterranean realm and returned "are not uncommon."[14] Thus the Departure—Initiation—Return cycle has not been borrowed wholesale from European mythology. Indeed, William Bascom's research shows that folktales which conclude as Tutuola's episode does, with the hero being transported back to the precise point where he began his adventures, are quite well known among the Yoruba.[15] All the evidence therefore seems to indicate that Tutuola was working well within the boundaries of traditional autochthonous verbal lore.

But what about the ghostess's hand? How do we explain the television set in her palm? Can this be said to be of African origin? Yes, I think it can, though we may have to look for its roots in African sorcery rather than in African oral art. If we search through published collections of African folktales for television motifs, we are likely to be disappointed unless we are willing to settle for analogues or hypothetical surrogates. Harold Collins has found an Ashanti tale "in which a young man has a magic mirror in his hand that allows him to see his home village when he is traveling"; this magic mirror is not unlike Tutuola's ghostly TV, but without further documentation—especially in Yoruba tales—one would be reluctant to accept the connection between the Ashanti mirror and Tutuola's tube as anything more than accidental.[16] However, when we switch channels and look at divination practices in West Africa, the picture becomes a lot clearer. Here is a firsthand account of an Ibo diviner at work.

When I was nine and not yet at school, I had the good fortune one morning as I passed by of being invited in by a diviner who lived only a few hundred yards away from my home. He beckoned me in to a dimly lit room. At one corner of it, a little away from a middle aged woman who sat anxiously on a low stool, was a normal size earthen pot, weirdly decorated with cowries, white sand, Kola nuts, and other odds and ends. The diviner ordered me to kneel before the pot and look into it which I did. He then covered my head with a piece of white cloth and informed me that if I concentrated my attention on the centre of the limpid liquid therein, a small window would automatically open through which I would see the netherworld. To the questions posed by the worried woman, appropriate replies were expected to be communicated by the denizens of the underworld through me as the medium. I obeyed the diviner's instructions, half in curiosity and half in fear. But as hard as I concentrated I saw nothing and I heard nothing.

The supernatural television did not work and, in honesty to my conscience, I confessed to the old man that there was no reply for me to relay on any of the questions put to the oracle. Disappointed at my naivety, the diviner reassured the woman of the potency of his oracle, and he claimed that it was the witchcraft in me which rendered it inactive that morning.[17]

This recourse to "supernatural television" to communicate with "denizens of the underworld" can also be found in Yoruba culture. E. Bolaji Idowu, a Yoruba theologian, points out that "the Yoruba believe that the deceased can be seen in dreams or trances, and that they can impart information or explanation, or give instructions, on any matters about which the family is in a serious predicament. They can also send messages through other persons or through certain cults to their folk."[18] Moreover, Geoffrey Parrinder, in his book on *West African Religion*, notes that throughout West Africa "it is believed that the soul of a dead person may be consulted anywhere from the hour of death, regardless of the place of death,"[19] and spiritualistic séances are frequently arranged to facilitate this communication.

Séances and visions of other worlds are not, of course, uniquely African, but in the mid-twentieth century the average African may be exposed to them much more frequently than the average European or American. Certainly Tutuola must have been familiar with the magical practices and divination lore of his own tribe. And since we have reliable evidence that he created the television-handed ghostess without ever having seen a television set in operation,[20] it is no doubt safe to assume that his fabrication of the ghostess's transcendental hand was inspired more by the Yoruba folk belief in the ability of professional diviners to magically tune in on a distant spirit world than it was by Western electronic technology. Tutuola was still operating entirely within a traditional African metaphysical system. He did not change *Weltanschauungs* in the middle of his stream of narrative.

The moral of this paper should be obvious. It is not "a spook in hand is worth two in the African bush" or "NBC is the mother of invention." Rather, it is nearer to the Yoruba proverb "A ki ifi ẹjẹ dudu sinu ki a tu itọ funfun jade," which means, "One does not have black blood inside and spit out white

[69]

saliva."[21] Amos Tutuola is a black writer who does not spew forth white culture. He may be a literary freak but he must be recognized as a thoroughly African one.

NOTES

1 One of the first critics to call Tutuola a freak was V. S. Pritchett, who reviewed Tutuola's second book, *My Life in the Bush of Ghosts*, in the *New Statesman and Nation*, March 6, 1954, p. 291. Gerald Moore expanded on the idea in his influential essay "Amos Tutuola," published originally in *Black Orpheus*, No. 1 (1957), pp. 27–35, and reprinted in Moore's *Seven African Writers* (London, 1962), pp. 39–57. For further discussion of Tutuola's critical reception, see my "Amos Tutuola and His Critics," *Abbia*, No. 22 (1969), pp. 109–18.

2 For discussion of Tutuola's debt to oral tradition, see E. N. Obiechina, "Amos Tutuola and the Oral Tradition," *Présence Africaine*, No. 65 (1968), pp. 85–106; Harold R. Collins, *Amos Tutuola* (New York, 1969), pp. 53–68; and my "Amos Tutuola's *The Palm-Wine Drinkard* and Oral Tradition," *Critique*, 11 (1968–69), 42–50, reprinted in the preceding chapter.

3 See Moore, *Seven African Writers*, p. 42.

4 See my "Amos Tutuola and D. O. Fagunwa," *Journal of Commonwealth Literature*, No. 9 (1970), pp. 57–65, and "Amos Tutuola: Debts and Assets," *Cahiers d'Etudes Africaines*, No. 38 (1970), pp. 306–34.

5 Robert P. Armstrong has attempted to define Tutuola's Yorubaness in "The Narrative and Intensive Continuity: *The Palm-Wine Drinkard*," *Research in African Literatures*, 1, No. 1 (1970), 9–34.

6 Amos Tutuola, *My Life in the Bush of Ghosts* (London, 1954). All quotations have been taken from this edition.

7 A. Olubummo, "D. O. Fagunwa—A Yoruba Novelist," *Odu*, No. 9 (September 1963), p. 26.

8 Tutuola's first book was *The Palm-Wine Drinkard and His Dead Palm-Wine Tapster in the Deads' Town* (London, 1952).

9 "Conversation with Amos Tutuola," *Africa Report*, 9, No. 7 (July 1964), 11.

10 This incident appears in Daniel O. Fagunwa's first book, *Ogboju Ode Ninu Igbo Irunmale* (London, 1938), which has recently been

translated by Wole Soyinka as *The Forest of a Thousand Daemons: A Hunter's Saga* (London, 1968). All quotations are taken from this translation.

11 The licking of repulsive, oozing sores is a common motif in African folktales, especially tales of the "Frau Holle" type (AT480), according to Alice Werner, "African Mythology," *The Mythology of All Races*, Vol. 7, ed. J. A. MacCullock (New York, 1964), p. 204. For an example of a Chaga tale with this motif, see Ojo Arewa's unpublished doctoral dissertation, "A Classification of the Folktales of the Northern East African Cattle Area by Types" (Berkeley, 1966), p. 183. In his *Motif-Index of Folk-Literature* (Bloomington, 1955–58), Stith Thompson lists under 041.2—"Reward for cleansing loathsome person"—an example from Leo Frobenius, *Atlantis: Volksdichtung und Volksmärchen Afrikas*, Vol. X (Jena, 1921–28), p. 242. Melville and Frances Herskovits record an example of this motif in an *enfant terrible* tale in *Dahomean Narrative* (Evanston, 1958), p. 294.

12 "Characteristics of Yoruba and Ibo Prose Styles in English," the last chapter in this book. Cf. Armstrong, "Narrative and Intensive Continuity."

13 Moore, pp. 50–51.

14 Werner, "African Mythology," pp. 118, 184.

15 I am grateful to Professor Bascom for allowing me to examine his unpublished notes on Yoruba folktales. He has found three examples of this kind of folktale; Melville J. and Frances S. Herskovits, "Tales in Pidgin English from Nigeria," *Journal of American Folklore*, 44 (1931), 457–59; Barbara K. and Warren S. Walker, eds., *Nigerian Folk Tales* (New Brunswick, N.J., 1961), pp. 19–21; and Alfred Reuss, "Märchen der Wazeguha," *Mitteilungen des Seminars für Orientalische Sprachen Afrikanische Studien*, 34 (1931), 119. The latter reference, a Zigula rather than Yoruba tale, is summarized in Arewa's dissertation, pp. 207–09.

16 Collins, *Amos Tutuola*, p. 63. Since writing this, I have been informed by Professor Bascom that more than thirty versions of this tale (a variant of AT653A—known in Europe as a dilemma tale, "The Rarest Thing in the World") have been found in sub-Saharan Africa, some of them from peoples as diverse and widely separated as the Vai, Bulu, Ovimbundu, Tsonga, Swahili and Betsimisaraka. It is conceivable that a Yoruba version exists but has not yet been recorded.

17 A. Y. Eke, review of Geoffrey Parrinder's *Witchcraft* in *Ibadan*, N.S. No. 3 (June 1968), p. 33.

18 E. Bolaji Idowu, *Olódùmarè: God in Yoruba Belief* (London, 1962), p. 191.

19 Geoffrey Parrinder, *West African Religion: A Study of the Beliefs and Practices of Akan, Ewe, Yoruba, Ibo and Kindred Peoples* (London, 1961), p. 150.

20 Geoffrey Parrinder, "Foreword" to *My Life in the Bush of Ghosts*, p. 12.

21 This proverb is listed in Isaac O. Delano, *Owe l'Esin Oro: Yoruba Proverbs—Their Meaning and Usage* (Ibadan, 1966), p. 1. When Yoruba use this proverb, it has a somewhat different meaning: i.e., "It is better to speak one's mind rather than dissemble one's feelings. It is not good to pretend to love someone we hate." I have taken the same kind of liberty with it as Tutuola sometimes takes when utilizing English proverbs.

THE PALM-OIL WITH WHICH
ACHEBE'S WORDS ARE EATEN

Among the Ibo the art of conversation is regarded very highly,
and proverbs are the palm-oil with which words are eaten.
CHINUA ACHEBE

Chinua Achebe is a writer well known throughout Africa and
even beyond. His fame rests on solid personal achievements. As
a young man of twenty-eight he brought honor to his native
Nigeria by writing *Things Fall Apart*, the first novel of unques-
tioned literary merit from English-speaking West Africa. Critics
tend to agree that no African novelist writing in English has yet
surpassed Achebe's achievement in *Things Fall Apart*, except
perhaps Achebe himself. It was published in 1958 and Achebe
has written three novels and won several literary prizes since.
During this time his reputation has grown like a bush-fire in the
harmattan. Today he is regarded by many as Africa's finest
novelist.

If ever a man of letters deserved his success, that man is
Achebe. He is a careful and fastidious artist in full control of his
art, a serious craftsman who disciplines himself not only to write
regularly but to write well. He has that sense of decorum, pro-
portion and design lacked by too many contemporary novelists,
African and non-African alike. He is also a committed writer,
one who believes that it is his duty to serve his society. He feels
that the fundamental theme with which African writers should
concern themselves is

> that African peoples did not hear of culture for the first time from
> Europeans; that their societies were not mindless but frequently
> had a philosophy of great depth and value and beauty, that they
> had poetry and, above all, they had dignity.[1]

Each of Achebe's novels[2] sheds light on a different era in the

[73]

recent history of Nigeria. *Things Fall Apart* (1958) is set in a traditional Ibo village community at the turn of the century when the first European missionaries and administrative officials were beginning to penetrate inland. In *Arrow of God* (1964) the action takes place in a similar environment about twenty-five years later, the major difference being that the missionaries and district officers have by this time become quite firmly entrenched. Achebe switches to an urban scene in *No Longer at Ease* (1960) in order to present a picture of the life of an educated Nigerian in the late nineteen-fifties. He brings the historical record right up to contemporary times in *A Man of the People* (1966), a devastating political satire that ends with a military coup. Achebe's novels read like chapters in a biography of his people and his nation since the coming of the white man.

What gives each of Achebe's novels an air of historical authenticity is his use of the English language. He has developed not one prose style but several, and in each novel he is careful to select the style or styles that will best suit his subject. In dialogue, for example, a Westernized African character will never speak exactly like a European character nor will he speak like an illiterate village elder. Achebe, a gifted ventriloquist, is able to individualize his characters by differentiating their speech. Of course, any sensitive novelist will try to do this, but most novelists do not face the problem of having to represent in English the utterances of a character who is speaking another language. To resolve this problem, Achebe has devised an African vernacular style[3] which simulates the idiom of Ibo, his native tongue. One example of this style will suffice. In *Arrow of God* a chief priest tells one of his sons why it is necessary to send him to a mission school:

> "I want one of my sons to join these people and be my eye there. If there is nothing in it you will come back. But if there is something there you will bring home my share. The world is like a Mask dancing. If you want to see it well you do not stand in one place. My spirit tells me that those who do not befriend the white man today will be saying *had we known* tomorrow." (p. 55)

In an article on "English and the African Writer," Achebe demonstrates that he could have written this passage in a different style:

> I am sending you as my representative among those people—just to be on the safe side in case the new religion develops. One has to move with the times or else one is left behind. I have a hunch that those who fail to come to terms with the white man may well regret their lack of foresight. [4]

Achebe comments, "The material is the same. But the form of the one is *in character* and the other is not. It is largely a matter of instinct, but judgement comes into it too."[5]

Achebe's use of an African vernacular style is not limited to dialogue. In *Things Fall Apart* and *Arrow of God*, novels set in tribal society, the narrative itself is studded with proverbs and similes which help to evoke the cultural milieu in which the action takes place. In *No Longer at Ease* and *A Man of the People*, on the other hand, one finds the language of the narrative more cosmopolitan, more Westernized, more suited to life in the city. Here are some similes drawn from narrative portions of *Things Fall Apart* (TFA) and *Arrow of God* (AOG):

. . . like a bush-fire in the harmattan. (TFA, p. 1)
. . . like pouring grains of corn into a bag full of holes. (TFA, p. 19)
. . . as if water had been poured on the tightened skin of a drum. (TFA, p. 42)
. . . like a yam tendril in the rainy season. (TFA, p. 45)
. . . like the snapping of a tightened bow. (TFA, p. 53)
. . . as busy as an ant-hill. (TFA, p. 100)
. . . like the walk of an Ijele Mask lifting and lowering each foot with weighty ceremony. (AOG, p. 84)
. . . like a grain of maize in an empty goatskin bag. (AOG, p. 100)
. . . as one might pull out a snail from its shell. (AOG, p. 118)
. . . like a bad cowry. (AOG, p. 146)
. . . like a lizard fallen from an iroko tree. (AOG, p. 242)
. . . like the blue, quiet, razor-edge flame of burning palm-nut shells. (AOG, p. 274)

Now here are some similes drawn from narrative portions of *No Longer at Ease* (NLAE) and *A Man of the People* (AMOP):

. . . as a collector fixes his insect with formalin. (NLAE, p. 1)

. . . swivelling their hips as effortlessly as oiled ball-bearings. (NLAE, p. 18)

. . . like a giant tarmac from which God's aeroplane might take off. (NLAE, p. 24)

. . . like an enchanted isle. (NLAE, p. 28)

. . . like the jerk in the leg of a dead frog when a current is applied to it. (NLAE, p. 137)

. . . like a panicky fly trapped behind the windscreen. (NLAE, p. 149)

. . . as a dentist extracts a stinking tooth. (AMOP, p. 4)

. . . like that radio jingle advertising an intestinal worm expeller. (AMOP, p. 29)

. . . as I had been one day, watching for the first time the unveiling of the white dome of Kilimanjaro at sunset. (AMOP, p. 45)

. . . as those winged termites driven out of the earth by late rain dance furiously around street lamps and then drop panting to the ground. (AMOP, p. 51)

. . . like a slowed up action film. (AMOP, p. 145)

. . . like a dust particle in the high atmosphere around which the water vapour of my thinking formed its globule of rain. (AMOP, p. 146)

In the urban novels one also finds similes drawn from village life, but in the novels set entirely in tribal society one finds no similes drawn from urban experience. This is altogether fitting, for Achebe's urban characters have lived in villages, but most of the characters of his village novels have had little or no exposure to cities. Here again we see Achebe using judgment and instinct to select the type of imagery that is appropriate to the time, place and people he is trying to picture. It is Achebe's sensitive use of appropriate language that lends an air of historicity to his novels.

I have taken time to comment on Achebe's artistry because the argument I intend to pursue is based on the premise that Achebe is an exceptional literary artist. I believe that he is both a conscious and an unconscious artist, that he has an instinct for knowing where things belong and a talent for putting them there, and that he possesses a shrewd sense of what is *in character* and what is not. All these qualities are displayed in his deliberate

[76]

search for an appropriate language for each novel, a style that will not only suit his subject and evoke the right cultural milieu but will also help to define the moral issues with which the novel is concerned.

It is my contention that Achebe, a skillful artist, achieves an appropriate language for each of his novels largely through the use of proverbs. Indeed, Achebe's proverbs can serve as keys to an understanding of his novels because he uses them not merely to add touches of local color but to sound and reiterate themes, to sharpen characterization, to clarify conflict, and to focus on the values of the society he is portraying. Proverbs thus provide a "grammar of values"[6] by which the deeds of a hero can be measured and evaluated. By studying Achebe's proverbs we are better able to interpret his novels.

Things Fall Apart is the story of Okonkwo, a famous warrior and expert farmer who has risen from humble origins to become a wealthy and respected leader of his clan. His entire life has been a struggle to achieve status, and he has almost attained a position of preeminence when he accidentally kills a kinsman. For this crime he must leave his clan and live in exile for seven years. When he returns at the end of the seventh year, he finds that things have changed in his home village. White missionaries have established a church and have made a number of converts. White men have also set up a court where the district commissioner comes to judge cases according to a foreign code of law. Okonkwo tries to rouse his clan to take action against these foreigners and their institutions. In a rage he kills one of the district commissioner's messengers. When his clan does not support his action, he commits suicide.

Okonkwo is pictured throughout the novel as a wrestler. It is an appropriate image not just because he is a powerful brute of a man and a renowned wrestler, not just because his life has been a ceaseless struggle for status, but because in the eyes of his people he brings about his own downfall by challenging too powerful an adversary. This adversary is not the white man, but rather Okonkwo's *chi*, his personal god or guardian spirit.[7]

Okonkwo is crushed because he tries to wrestle with his *chi*. The Ibo have a folktale about just such a wrestler.

> Once there was a great wrestler whose back had never known the ground. He wrestled from village to village until he had thrown every man in the world. Then he decided that he must go and wrestle in the land of spirits, and become champion there as well. He went, and beat every spirit that came forward. Some had seven heads, some ten; but he beat them all. His companion who sang his praise on the flute begged him to come away, but he would not. He pleaded with him but his ear was nailed up. Rather than go home he gave a challenge to the spirits to bring out their best and strongest wrestler. So they sent him his personal god, a little, wiry spirit who seized him with one hand and smashed him on the stony earth. [8]

Although this tale does not appear in *Things Fall Apart*, there is sufficient evidence in the novel to suggest that Okonkwo is being likened to one who dares to wrestle with a spirit. A hint is contained in the first paragraph of the opening chapter which tells how Okonkwo gained fame as a young man of eighteen by throwing an unbeaten wrestler "in a fight which the old men agreed was one of the fiercest since the founder of their town engaged a spirit of the wild for seven days and seven nights." (p. 1) And later, when Okonkwo commits the sin of beating one of his wives during the sacred Week of Peace, ". . . people said he had no respect for the gods of his clan. His enemies said his good fortune had gone to his head. They called him the little bird *nza* who so far forgot himself after a heavy meal that he challenged his *chi*." (p. 26)

Achebe uses proverbs to reinforce the image of Okonkwo as a man who struggles with his *chi*. Notice in the following passage how skillfully this is done:

> Everybody at the kindred meeting took sides with Osugo when Okonkwo called him a woman. The oldest man present said sternly that those whose palm-kernels were cracked for them by a benevolent spirit should not forget to be humble. Okonkwo said he was sorry for what he had said, and the meeting continued.
> But it was really not true that Okonkwo's palm-kernels had

been cracked for him by a benevolent spirit. He had cracked them himself. Anyone who knew his grim struggle against poverty and misfortune could not say he had been lucky. If ever a man deserved his success, that man was Okonkwo. At an early age he had achieved fame as the greatest wrestler in all the land. That was not luck. At the most one could say that his *chi* or personal god was good. But the Ibo people have a proverb that when a man says yes his *chi* also says yes. Okonkwo said yes very strongly; so his *chi* agreed. And not only his *chi* but his clan too, because it judged a man by the work of his hands. (pp. 22–23)

When Okonkwo returns from exile, he makes the mistake of believing that if he says yes strongly enough, his *chi* and his clan will agree. No doubt he should have known better. He should have accepted his years in exile as a warning from his *chi*. In his first months of exile he had come close to understanding the truth:

Clearly his personal god or *chi* was not made for great things. A man could not rise beyond the destiny of his *chi*. The saying of the elders was not true—that if a man said yea his *chi* also affirmed. Here was a man whose *chi* said nay despite his own affirmation. (p. 117)

However, as the years of exile pass, Okonkwo's fortunes improve and he begins to feel "that his *chi* might now be making amends for the past disaster." (p. 154) He returns to his clan rich, confident, and eager to resume his former position of leadership. When he finds his village changed, he tries to transform it into the village it had once been. But although he says yes very strongly, his *chi* and his clan say nay. Okonkwo the wrestler is at last defeated.

Quite a few of the proverbs that Achebe uses in *Things Fall Apart* are concerned with status and achievement:

. . . the sun will shine on those who stand before it shines on those who kneel under them. (p. 5)
. . . if a child washed his hands he could eat with kings. (p. 6)
. . . a man who pays respect to the great paves the way for his own greatness. (p. 16)
The lizard that jumped from the high iroko tree to the ground said he would praise himself if no one else did. (p. 18)

. . . you can tell a ripe corn by its look. (p. 18)
I cannot live on the bank of a river and wash my hands with
    spittle. (p. 148)
.. . as a man danced so the drums were beaten for him. (p. 165)

Such proverbs tell us much about the values of Ibo society,
values by which Okonkwo lives and dies. Such proverbs also
serve as thematic statements reminding us of some of the major
motifs in the novel—e.g., the importance of status, the value of
achievement, the idea of man as shaper of his own destiny.

Sometimes in Achebe's novels one finds proverbs expressing
different views on the same subject. Examined closely, these
proverbs can provide clues to significant differences in outlook
or opinion which set one man apart from others. For example,
there are a number of proverbs in *Things Fall Apart* comparing
parents and their children. Most Ibos believe that a child will
take after his parents, or as one character puts it, "When mother
cow is chewing grass its young ones watch its mouth." (p. 62)
However, Okonkwo's father had been a failure, and Okonkwo,
not wanting to be likened to him, had striven to make his own
life a success. So impressive were his achievements and so rapid
his rise that an old man was prompted to remark, "Looking at a
king's mouth, one would think he never sucked at his mother's
breast." (p. 22) Okonkwo believed that one's ancestry was not
as important as one's initiative and will power, qualities which
could be discerned in a child at a very early age. "A chick
that will grow into a cock," he said, "can be spotted the very
day it hatches." (p. 58) He had good reason for thinking so.
He himself had achieved much as a young man, but his own son
Nwoye had achieved nothing at all.

How could he have begotten a woman for a son? At Nwoye's age,
Okonkwo had already become famous throughout Umuofia for
his wrestling and his fearlessness.
    He sighed heavily, and as if in sympathy the smouldering log
also sighed. And immediately Okonkwo's eyes were opened and
he saw the whole matter clearly. Living fire begets cold, impotent
ash. He sighed again, deeply. (p. 138)

It is worth noting that in complaining about Nwoye's unmanliness, Okonkwo says, "A bowl of pounded yams can throw him in a wrestling match." (p. 57) All the proverbs cited here are working to characterize Okonkwo and to set him apart from other men, especially from his father and his son. The proverbs reveal that no one, least of all Okonkwo himself, considers him an ordinary mortal; rather, he is the sort of man who would dare to wrestle with his *chi*.

Obi Okonkwo, who is Okonkwo's grandson and the hero of Achebe's second novel, *No Longer at Ease*, is a very different kind of person. When he returns from studies in England, he is an honest, idealistic young man. He takes a high paying job in the civil service but soon finds that his salary is not sufficient to meet the financial demands made upon him. He also gets involved with a woman his parents and clan despise. In the end he is caught taking bribes and is sent to prison.

Obi is an unheroic figure, a good man who slides rather than falls into evil ways. His actions are ignoble and unworthy. When he begins taking bribes, he tries to satisfy his conscience by refusing to take them from people he knows he cannot help. Kinsmen who attend his trial cannot understand why he took such risks for so little profit; one says, "I am against people reaping where they have not sown. But we have a saying that if you want to eat a toad you should look for a fat and juicy one." (p. 6) But Obi lives by half measures, by resolute decisions mollified by irresolute actions. He falls in love with Clara, a woman whose unusual ancestry Obi's parents look upon with horror, and he wants to marry her. A friend warns him not to pollute his lineage: "What you are going to do concerns not only yourself but your whole family and future generations. If one finger brings oil it soils the others." (p. 75) Obi, feeling he must free himself from the shackles of tradition, becomes engaged to Clara but later yields to parental pressure and breaks off with her. When she reveals she is pregnant, he arranges for her to get an abortion. More shameful, at least in the eyes of his clan, is Obi's refusal to return home for his mother's funeral, an action that leads one dismayed clansman to suggest that Obi is rotten at the core: "A man may go to England, become a lawyer or doctor, but it does not change his blood. It is like a bird that flies off the earth and lands on an ant-hill. It is still on the ground." (p. 160) Obi never gets off the ground, never reaches heroic heights, never stops swallowing undernourished toads.

Helping to set the tone of the story are a great number of proverbs which comment on or warn against foolish and unworthy actions. Besides those already mentioned, one finds:

He that fights for a ne'er-do-well has nothing to show for it except a head covered in earth and grime. (p. 5)

The fox must be chased away first; after that the hen might be warned against wandering into the bush. (p. 5)

. . . he replied that a man who lived on the banks of the Niger should not wash his hands with spittle. (pp. 10, 135)

. . . like the young antelope who danced herself lame when the main dance was yet to come. (p. 11)

When a new saying gets to the land of empty men they lose their heads over it. (p. 48)

A person who has not secured a place on the floor should not begin to look for a mat. (p. 60)

Shall we kill a snake and carry it in our hand when we have a bag for putting long things in? (p. 80)

. . . digging a new pit to fill up an old one. (p. 108)

. . . a man should not, out of pride and etiquette, swallow his phlegm. (p. 156)

. . . The little bird *nza* who after a big meal so far forgot himself as to challenge his *chi* to single combat. (p. 163)

A man does not challenge his *chi* to a wrestling match. (p. 40)

The last two proverbs cited here may remind us of Okonkwo, but no one could mistake Obi for his grandfather. Okonkwo erred by daring to attempt something he did not have the power to achieve; this makes him a tragic hero. Obi erred by stooping to take bribes; this makes him a crook. To put it in proverbial terms: Okonkwo wrestles his *chi*, Obi swallows a toad. It is not only the stupidity but the contemptibility of Obi's ways that many of the proverbs in the novel help to underscore.

[82]

An important theme in *No Longer at Ease* is the conflict between old and new values. Obi's people tax themselves merci-
lessly to raise funds to send him to England for university training. The "scholarship" they award him is to be repaid both in
cash and in services when he finishes his studies. They want him
to read law so that when he returns he will be able to handle all
their land cases against their neighbors. They expect a good
return on their investment because Obi is their kinsman; they
have a saying that ". . . he who has people is richer than he who
has money." (p. 79) Obi, however, immediately asserts his self-
will by choosing to read English instead of law. When he returns
he starts to pay back the loan but refuses to allow his kinsmen to
interfere in his personal life. He especially resents their efforts to
dissuade him from marrying Clara. Having adopted Western
values, Obi believes that an individual has the right to choose
his own wife. It is this that brings him into conflict with his
parents and kinsmen. Obi's Western education has made him an
individualist, but his people still adhere to communal values.[9]

Obi's people attach great importance to kinship ties, and their
beliefs regarding the obligations and rewards of kinship are often
revealed in their proverbs. Even when a prodigal son like Obi
gets into trouble, they feel it is necessary to try to help him: ". . .
a kinsman in trouble had to be saved, not blamed; anger against
a brother was felt in the flesh, not in the bone." (p. 5) They also
have a song which cautions:

> He that has a brother must hold him to his heart,
> For a kinsman cannot be bought in the market,
> Neither is a brother bought with money. (p. 129)

Certainly it would be very wrong to harm an in-law for ". . . a
man's in-law was his *chi*." (p. 46) And conflict within the clan
should be avoided, for in unity lies strength: "If all snakes lived
together in one place, who would approach them?" (p. 81)
Those who prosper are expected to help those who are less for-
tunate: ". . . when there is a big tree small ones climb on its
back to reach the sun." (p. 96) But all the burdens should
not fall on one man: ". . . it is not right to ask a man with

elephantiasis of the scrotum to take on small pox as well, when thousands of other people have not had even their share of small diseases." (p. 99) Obi accepts some of the values expressed in these proverbs, but his own individualistic attitude is probably best summed up in the saying "Ours is ours but mine is mine." (p. 32) Obi's problem lies in having to make choices between the old values and the new, between "ours" and "mine."

Ezeulu, hero of Achebe's third novel, *Arrow of God*, is faced with a similar problem. As chief priest of a snake cult Ezeulu is committed to traditional ways, but just to be on the safe side he sends one of his sons to a mission school to "be [his] eye there" and to learn the white man's ways. This action draws criticism from some of the leaders of the clan, criticism which rapidly mounts into angry protest when the Christianized son is caught trying to kill a sacred python. Ezeulu also falls afoul of the district officer by declining to accept an official appointment as paramount chief of his village. For this he is thrown into prison for two months. When he returns to his village he envisions himself as an avenging arrow in the bow of his god, an instrument by which his god intends to punish his people. Ezeulu therefore refuses to perform certain rituals which must be performed before new yams can be harvested. This precipitates a crisis which results in the destruction of Ezeulu, his priesthood and his religion.

To understand Ezeulu one must comprehend his deep concern over the way his world is changing. This concern is expressed both in his decision to send one of his sons to a mission school and in the proverbs he uses to justify his decision. He tells his son that a man must move with the times: ". . . I am like the bird Eneke-nti-oba. When his friends asked him why he was always on the wing he replied: 'Men of today have learnt to shoot without missing and so I have learnt to fly without perching.' . . . The world is like a Mask dancing. If you want to see it well you do not stand in one place." (p. 55) Months later Ezeulu reminds his son that he must learn the white man's magic because "a man must dance the dance prevalent in his time."

(p. 234) Ezeulu explains his decision to the village elders by comparing the white man to a new disease: "A disease that has never been seen before cannot be cured with everyday herbs. When we want to make a charm we look for the animal whose blood can match its power; if a chicken cannot do it we look for a goat or a ram; if that is not sufficient we send for a bull. But sometimes even a bull does not suffice, then we must look for a human." (p. 165) Ezeulu's son is to be the human sacrifice which will enable the clan to make medicine of sufficient strength to hold the new disease in check. In other words, Ezeulu decides to sacrifice his son in order to gain power to cope with the changing times.

The question is whether Ezeulu's action is an appropriate response to the problem. Some elders think it is not and blame Ezeulu for bringing new trouble to the village by taking so improper a step. The importance that Ezeulu's people attach to appropriate action is reflected in many of the proverbs in the novel. For example:

> If the lizard of the homestead neglects to do the things for which its kind is known, it will be mistaken for the lizard of the farmland. (pp. 20–21)
> . . . let us first chase away the wild cat, afterwards we blame the hen. (p. 122)
> We do not by-pass a man and enter his compound. (p. 138)
> We do not apply an ear-pick to the eye. (p. 138)
> . . . bale that water before it rises above the ankle. (pp. 156, 197)
> When a masked spirit visits you you have to appease its footprints with presents. (p. 190)
> . . . a traveller to distant places should make no enemies. (p. 208)
> . . . a man of sense does not go on hunting little bush rodents when his age mates are after big game. (p. 209)
> He who sees an old hag squatting should leave her alone; who knows how she breathes? (p. 282)

Sending a son to a mission school is regarded by some elders as a highly inappropriate action for a chief priest to take, no matter what his motivation.

Ezeulu's enemies interpret his deed as a gesture of friendship toward the white man. Thus, when the district commissioner rather curtly commands Ezeulu to appear in his office within twenty-four hours and Ezeulu calls the elders together to ask if they think he should heed the summons, one unfriendly elder replies in no uncertain proverbs that Ezeulu must either suffer the consequences of friendship with the white man or do something to end the friendship:

". . . does Ezeulu think that their friendship should stop short of entering each other's houses? Does he want the white man to be his friend only by word of mouth? Did not our elders tell us that as soon as we shake hands with a leper he will want an embrace? . . . What I say is this . . . a man who brings ant-ridden faggots into his hut should expect the visit of lizards. But if Ezeulu is now telling us that he is tired of the white man's friendship our advice to him should be: You tied the knot, you should also know how to undo it. You passed the shit that is smelling; you should carry it away. Fortunately the evil charm brought in at the end of a pole is not too difficult to take outside again." (pp. 177–78)

It is worth noting that the proverb about bringing ant-ridden faggots home is quoted twice by Ezeulu himself. He uses it to reproach himself when his mission-educated son is found trying to kill a sacred python. (p. 72) Here, momentarily at least, Ezeulu seems willing to accept responsibility for the abomination. Ezeulu uses the proverb a second time when a friend accuses him of betraying his people by sending his son to the white man's school. Ezeulu counters by pointing out that he did not bring the white man to his people; rather, his people brought the white man upon themselves by failing to oppose him when he first arrived. If they wish to blame someone, they should blame themselves for meekly submitting to the white man's presence and power. "The man who brings ant-ridden faggots into his hut should not grumble when lizards begin to pay him a visit." (p. 163) This is a key proverb in *Arrow of God* for it enunciates a major theme: that a man is responsible for his actions and must bear their consequences.

But in addition to being responsible for his actions, a man is also expected to act responsibly. This idea is conveyed in another key proverb which is used four times in the novel: "... an adult does not sit and watch while the she-goat suffers the pain of childbirth tied to a post." (p. 258, cf. pp. 21, 31, 189) Ezeulu uses this proverb twice to reprimand elders for encouraging the village to fight a "war of blame" against a neighboring village. He reminds them that elders must not neglect their duty to their people by acting irresponsibly. It is quite significant that this same proverb is used later by the elders to rebuke Ezeulu for failing to perform the ritual that will permit new yams to be harvested. (p. 258) The' elders suggest that Ezeulu is doing nothing to prevent or relieve the suffering of his people. They urge him to do his duty by performing the necessary ritual. They urge him, in other words, to act responsibly.

Ezeulu answers that he has a higher responsibility, for his god, Ulu, has forbidden him to perform the ritual. The elders then say that if Ezeulu will perform the ritual, they themselves will take the blame for it: "... if Ulu says we have committed an abomination let it be on the heads of the ten of us here. You will be free because we have set you to it, and the person who sets a child to catch a shrew should also find him water to wash the odour from his hand. We shall find you the water." (p. 260) Ezeulu answers, "... you cannot say: do what is not done and we shall take the blame. I am the Chief Priest of Ulu and what I have told you is his will not mine." (pp. 260–61) Ezeulu sincerely believes that he is the instrument of a divine power, "an arrow in the bow of his god." (p. 241) When his actions bring disaster upon himself and his people, he does not feel responsible but rather feels betrayed by his god.

> Why, he asked himself again and again, why had Ulu chosen to deal thus with him, to strike him down and cover him with mud? What was his offence? Had he not divined the god's will and obeyed it? When was it ever heard that a child was scalded by the piece of yam its own mother put in its palm? What man would send his son with a potsherd to bring fire from a neighbour's hut and then unleash rain on him? Who ever sent his son up the palm to gather nuts and then took an axe and felled the tree? (p. 286)

Tortured by these questions, Ezeulu finally goes mad.

The elders come to regard Ezeulu as a man who brought tragedy upon himself by failing to recognize his own limitations. In order to act appropriately and responsibly, a man must know his limitations. This idea finds expression in many of the proverbs in the novel:

> . . . like the little bird, *nza*, who ate and drank and challenged his personal god to a single combat. (p. 17)
>
> . . . no matter how strong or great a man was he should never challenge his *chi*. (p. 32)
>
> The man who carries a deity is not a king. (p. 33)
>
> A man who knows that his anus is small does not swallow an udala seed. (pp. 87, 282)
>
> . . . only a foolish man can go after a leopard with his bare hands. (p. 105)
>
> The fly that struts around on a mound of excrement wastes his time; the mound will always be greater than the fly. (p. 282)

To sum up, Ezeulu, in trying to adjust to the changing times, takes certain inappropriate actions which later lead him to neglect his duties and responsibilities. Not knowing his limitations, he goes too far and plunges himself and his people into disaster.

Achebe's most recent novel, *A Man of the People*, is set in contemporary Nigeria and takes as its hero a young schoolteacher, Odili Samalu. Odili, who tells his own story, is moved to enter politics when his mistress is seduced by Chief the Honourable M. A. Nanga, M.P. and Minister of Culture. Odili joins a newly-formed political party and prepares to contest Nanga's seat in the next election. He also tries to win the affections of Nanga's fiancée, a young girl Nanga is grooming as his "parlour wife." In the end Odili loses the political battle but manages to win the girl. Nanga loses everything because the election is so rough and dirty and creates such chaos in the country that the Army stages a coup and imprisons every member of the Government.

In Nanga, Achebe has created one of the finest rogues in Nigerian fiction. Claiming to be a "man of the people," Nanga is actually a self-seeking, grossly corrupt politician who lives in flamboyant opulence on his ill-gotten gains. He is fond of pious platitudes—"Not what I have but what I do is my kingdom" (p. 3); "Do the right and shame the Devil" (p. 12)—but his ruthless drive for money and power is far from pious. When criticized, he accuses his critics of "character assassination" and answers that ". . . no one is perfect except God." (p. 75) He frequently complains of the troubles and burdens that Government Ministers have to bear and readily agrees when someone remarks, "Uneasy lies the head that wears the crown." (p. 68) Nanga has enormous power which he is willing to use to help others provided that they in turn help him. In a country in which "it didn't matter *what* you knew but *who* you knew," (p. 19) Nanga was obviously a man to know.

The maxims quoted here help to characterize Nanga and his world. They are sayings borrowed from a foreign culture and are as often misapplied and abused as are the manners and institutions which have also been borrowed from Europe and transplanted in contemporary Africa. Nanga quotes these maxims but does not live by them; similarly, he gives lip service to democratic elections but does everything in his power to subvert and manipulate them. Detribalized but imperfectly Westernized, adhering to no systematic code of values, Nanga battles to stay on top in a confused world. He is one of the most monstrous offspring produced by the tawdry union of Europe and Africa, and his misuse of non-African mottoes and maxims exposes not only his own insincerity and irresponsibility but the moral chaos in the world in which he lives.

Odili, a more thoroughly Westernized African, is a man of far greater virtue and integrity. His narrative is sprinkled with imported metaphors and proverbial expressions—e.g., "kicked the bucket," (p. 28) "pass through the eye of a needle," (p. 63) "one stone to kill two birds with," (p. 152) "attack . . . is the best defence," (p. 162) "a bird in the hand" (p. 165)—but he always uses them appropriately. Whatever he says can be trusted to be accurate and honest. Somehow Odili has managed to remain untainted amidst all the surrounding corruption and his clear vision provides an undistorted view of a warped society.

Contemporary Nigeria is, after all, the real subject of the novel. What sort of society is it that allows men like Nanga to thrive while men like Odili suffer? Some important clues are provided in the proverbs in the novel. In contemporary Nigeria one must, for example, be circumspect:

> . . . the proverbial traveller-to-distant-places who must not culti-vate enmity on his route. (p. 1)
> . . . when one slave sees another cast into a shallow grave he should know that when the time comes he will go the same way. (p. 40)
> . . . if you respect today's king, others will respect you when your turn comes. (p. 70)
> . . . if you look only in one direction your neck will become stiff. (p. 90)

But one must not be unduly inquisitive:

> . . . naked curiosity—the kind that they say earned Monkey a bullet in the forehead. (p. 153)
> The inquisitive eye will only blind its own sight. (p. 164)
> A man who insists on peeping into his neighbour's bedroom know-ing a woman to be there is only punishing himself. (p. 164)

One should take advantage of opportunities (". . . if you fail to take away a strong man's sword when he is on the ground, will you do it when he gets up . . .?" p. 103); capitalize on good fortune ("[would] a sensible man . . . spit out the juicy morsel that good fortune placed in his mouth?" p. 2); and avoid wasting time on trivialities (". . . like the man in the proverb who was carrying the carcass of an elephant on his head and searching with his toes for a grasshopper" p. 80). Most important of all, one must be sure to get one's share. Like the world of Obi Okonkwo in *No Longer at Ease*, this is a world in which "ours is ours but mine is mine." (p. 140)

One must not only get one's share, one must also consume it. Eating is an important image in the novel. Politicians like Nanga tell their tribesmen, "Our people must press for their fair share of the national cake." (p. 13) Those who stand in the way of such hungry politicians are branded as "the hybrid class of Western-educated and snobbish intellectuals who will not hesitate to sell their mothers for a mess of pottage." (p. 6) These intellectuals, Nanga says, "have bitten the finger with which their mother fed them." (p. 6) Although some people believe that God will provide for everyone according to His will ("He holds the knife and He holds the yam," p. 102), the politicians know that the fattest slices of the national cake together with the richest icing will go to the politicians who hold the most power. This is the reason elections are so hotly contested. In these elections people are quite willing to support a corrupt politician like Nanga in the belief that if he remains well fed, he may let a few crumbs fall to his constituents. When someone like Odili protests that such politicians are using their positions to enrich themselves, the people answer cynically, "Let them eat, . . . after all when white men used to do all the eating did we commit suicide?" (p. 161) Besides, who can tell what the future may bring? ". . . who knows? It may be your turn to eat tomorrow. Your son may bring home your share." (p. 162) It is not surprising that Odili sums up this era as a "fat-dripping, gummy, eat-and-let-eat regime . . . a regime which inspired the common saying that a man could only be sure of what he had put away safely in his gut or, in language ever more suited to the times: 'you chop, me self I chop, palaver finish.' " (p. 167)

The reason such an era comes to an end is that the politicians make the mistake of overeating, of taking more than their share. In proverbial terms, they take more than the owner can ignore. This key proverb is used four times in the novel. Twice it is applied to a miserly trader who steals a blind man's stick: "Josiah has taken away enough for the owner to notice," people say in disgust. "Josiah has now removed enough for the owner to see him." (p. 97) Odili later reflects on the situation and the proverb:

> I thought much afterwards about that proverb, about the man taking things away until the owner at last notices. In the mouth of our people there was no greater condemnation. It was not just a

simple question of a man's cup being full. A man's cup might be full and none the wiser. But here the owner knew, and the owner, I discovered, is the will of the whole people. (p. 97)

In the middle of his campaign against Nanga, Odili wishes that "someone would get up and say: 'No, Nanga has taken more than the owner could ignore!'" (p. 122) But it is only after much post-election violence and an army takeover that Odili's wish comes true. Only after such upheavals result in the establishment of a new order do people openly admit that Nanga and his cohorts "had taken enough for the owner to see." (p. 166)

Thus, in *A Man of the People*, as in Achebe's other novels, proverbs are used to sound and reiterate major themes, to sharpen characterization, to clarify conflict, and to focus on the values of the society Achebe is portraying. By studying the proverbs in a novel, we gain insight into the moral issues with which that novel deals. Because they provide a *grammar of values* by which the actions of characters can be measured and evaluated, proverbs help us to understand and interpret Achebe's novels.

Achebe's literary talents are clearly revealed in his use of proverbs. One can observe his mastery of the English language, his skill in choosing the right words to convey his ideas, his keen sense of what is *in character* and what is not, his instinct for appropriate metaphor and symbol, and his ability to present a thoroughly African world in thoroughly African terms. It is this last talent that enables him to convince his readers "that African peoples did not hear of culture for the first time from Europeans; that their societies were not mindless but frequently had a philosophy of great depth and value and beauty, that they had poetry and, above all, they had dignity."[10]

NOTES

1 Chinua Achebe, "The Role of the Writer in a New Nation," *Nigeria Magazine*, No. 81 (June 1964), p. 157.

2 Chinua Achebe, *Things Fall Apart* (London, 1958); *No Longer at Ease* (London, 1960); *Arrow of God* (London, 1964); *A Man of the People* (London, 1966). All quotations are from these editions.

3 I discuss this at more length in "African Vernacular Styles in Nigerian Fiction," *CLA Journal*, 9 (1966), 265–73. See also Gerald Moore, "English Words, African Lives," *Présence Africaine*, No. 54 (1965), pp. 90–101; Ezekiel Mphahlele, "The Language of African Literature," *Harvard Educational Review*, 34 (Spring 1964), 298–305; and Eldred Jones, "Language and Theme in *Things Fall Apart*," *Review of English Literature*, 5, No. 4 (October 1964), 39–43.

4 *Transition*, No. 18 (1965), p. 30. The same article appears in *Moderna Språk*, 58 (1964), 438–46.

5 *Ibid.*

6 I have borrowed this phrase from M. J. Herskovits, who once said, ". . . the total corpus of the proverbs of Africans, as with proverb-users in other societies, is in a very real sense their grammar of values." *Dahomean Narrative* (Evanston, 1958), p. 56. For another discussion of Achebe's proverbs, see Austin J. Shelton, "The 'Palm-Oil' of Language: Proverbs in Chinua Achebe's Novels," *Modern Language Quarterly*, 30, No. 1 (1969), 86–111.

7 There has been some controversy about the meaning of "chi." See Austin J. Shelton, "The Offended *chi* in Achebe's Novels," *Transition*, No. 13 (1964), pp. 36–37, and Donatus Nwoga, "The *chi* Offended," *Transition*, No. 15 (1964), p. 5. Shelton prefers to translate it as "God within," but Nwoga, an Ibo, supports Achebe's translation of it as "personal god." Victor Uchendu, an Ibo anthropologist, describes *chi* as "the Igbo form of guardian spirit" (*The Igbo of Southeast Nigeria*, New York, 1966, p. 16). I have followed Achebe and Uchendu here.

8 Quoted from Achebe's *Arrow of God*, pp. 31–32. A variant of this tale can be found in Cyprian Ekwensi, *Ikolo the Wrestler and Other Ibo Tales* (London, 1947), pp. 34–37. Another variant appears in F. Chidozie Ogbalu, *Niger Tales* (Aba, n.d.), pp. 9–11.

9 This theme is discussed by Obiajunwa Wali in "The Individual and the Novel in Africa," *Transition*, No. 18 (1965), pp. 31–33.

10 See footnote 1.

THE FOLKTALE AS PARADIGM IN CHINUA ACHEBE'S *ARROW OF GOD*

Toward the end of his third novel, *Arrow of God*, Chinua Achebe devotes five pages to the telling of a traditional Ibo folktale. On the surface this tale appears to have no bearing on the events in the novel itself. It seems merely a digression, an unnecessary detour into the folkways of a people who half a century ago had very little contact with the outside world. Many critics have dismissed such passages in Achebe's fiction as well-intentioned but artistically unjustified attempts to embroider a story with authentic bits of aboriginal local color. Achebe, they complain, gives the impression of being primarily a sociologist,[1] for his novels are "long on native customs and idiom, and short on narrative interest."[2] *Arrow of God*, his most ambitious work, is inevitably singled out for its copious "anthropological documentation," which makes it "perhaps too elaborate, too worked out, too insistent, and a little tendentious."[3] Though an impressive imaginative achievement, this novel, it is argued, ultimately fails to satisfy the reader esthetically because its "parts are not all, or do not appear to be, evolutionarily contingent one upon the other."[4]

The critics who make these remarks are usually European or American book reviewers who have little knowledge of traditional African modes of storytelling. They are not aware that Achebe, like many a fireside raconteur, often uses proverbs and folktales to comment indirectly on eccentricities of human behavior which have been observed or manifested recently by his audience. The lore thus serves a moral purpose, interpreting as well as reflecting contemporary social realities. In his four novels Achebe carries this technique a step further by making the folklore relate significantly not only to the real world of his

readers but also, more importantly, to the fictional world his
dramatis personae inhabit. His proverbs and folktales are not
exotic digressions but fully functional narrative progressions,
not superfluous anthropological data but meaningful metaphors
illuminating the special contexts in which they are set.[5] To
appreciate how subtly these forms are sometimes made to
operate, let us look closely at the five-page folktale in the latter
part of *Arrow of God*.[6]

This prize-winning novel is concerned with Iboland in the
nineteen-twenties and has as its hero a headstrong chief priest of
a snake cult who falls victim to the changing times and to his own
towering pride. Ezeulu, priest of Ulu, is professionally committed
to traditional ways, but just to be on the safe side he sends one of
his own sons to a mission school to "be [his] eye there" and to
learn the white man's ways. This action draws criticism from
some of the leaders of the clan, criticism which rapidly mounts
into angry protest when the Christianized son is caught trying to
kill a sacred python. Ezeulu also falls afoul of the British district
officer by declining to accept an official appointment as paramount chief of his village. For this he is thrown into prison for
two months. He sits there furious with the district officer and
vexed with his own clansmen for failing to respond to his
imprisonment with adequate strength of action or sentiment.
When he returns to his village he sees himself as an avenging
arrow in the bow of his god, an instrument by which his god
intends to punish his people. Ezeulu therefore refuses to perform
certain seasonal rituals which must be performed before new
yams can be harvested. This precipitates a crisis which results in
the destruction of Ezeulu, his priesthood and his deity. Traditional Ibo society consequently falls further apart.

Ezeulu's catastrophic mistake is to turn against his own
people. While sitting in prison he formulates his wrong-headed
scheme to delay the new yam harvest by denying it his blessing.
However, when he returns home and receives a hero's welcome,
he begins to relent and think of reconciliation. "Was it right,"
he asks himself, "that he should stretch his hand against all these

people who had shown so much concern for him during his exile
and since his return?" (p. 231) It is in this interim period between Ezeulu's release from prison and his refusal to perform the
necessary rituals, the very period during which Ezeulu is trying
to decide whether or not to punish his people as he had originally intended, that the folktale we are concerned with is told.

It is told by Ezeulu's youngest wife to two of her small children. Here is the entire tale:

> Once upon a time there was a man who had two wives. The senior
> wife had many children but the younger one had only one son.
> One day the man and his family went to work on their farm. This
> farm was at the boundary between the land of men and the land
> of spirits. Anyone going to work in this neighbourhood must hurry
> away at sunset because as soon as darkness came the spirits arrived
> to work on their own yam-fields.
>
> This man and his wives and children worked until the sun began
> to go down. They quickly gathered their hoes and matchets and
> baskets and set out for home. But on reaching home the son of the
> second wife discovered that he had left his flute in the farm and
> said he would go back for it. His mother pleaded with him not to
> go but he would not listen. His father warned him it would be
> certain death to go but he did not listen. When they were tired of
> pleading with him they let him go.
>
> He passed over seven rivers and through seven wilds before he
> reached the farm. When he got near he saw spirits bending over
> their work planting ghost-yams. They all stood up on his approach
> and regarded him with anger in their eyes.
>
> "Ta! Human boy!" barked the leader of the spirits. "What do
> you want?" He spoke through the nose. "Have you never heard
> that we are abroad at this time."
>
> "I have come to take the flute I forgot under that dead tree."
>
> "Flute? Will you recognize it if you see it?"
>
> The boy said yes. The leader of the spirits then produced a flute
> shining like yellow metal.
>
> "Is this it?"
>
> The boy said no. Then he produced another flute shining white
> like the *nut of the water of heaven.*
>
> "Is this it?" he asked, and the boy again said no.
>
> Finally he produced the boy's bamboo flute and asked if it was
> his and the boy smiled and said yes.

"Take it and blow for us."

The boy took his flute from the hand of the spirit and blew this song:

> Awful Spirit, undisputed
> Lord by night o'er this estate!
> Father warned me death awaited
> Men who ventured here so late;
> "Please, my son, please wait till morning!"
> Cried my mother. But her warning
> Wasted fell. For how was I to
> Lie awake and wait for dawn
> While my flute in damp and dew
> Lay forsaken and forlorn?

The spirits were delighted with the song and there was a general haw-haw-haw through their noses.

The leader of the spirits brought out two pots, one big and one small. Both pots were completely sealed.

"Take one of these," he said to the boy. He took the small one.

"When you reach home, call your mother and your father and break the pot in front of them." The boy thanked him.

"On your way home, if you hear *dum-dum* you must run into the bush; but if you hear *jam-jam* come back to the road."

On his way the boy heard *dum-dum* and ran into the bush. Then he heard *jam-jam* and came out again. He passed the seven rivers and the seven wilds and finally reached his father's compound. He called his father and his mother and broke the pot before them. Immediately the place was filled with every good thing: yellow metal, cloths and velvets, foods of all kinds, money, cows, goats and many other things of value.

The boy's mother filled a basket with gifts and sent to her husband's senior wife. But she was blind with envy and refused the gift. She did not see why she should be insulted with a meagre present when all she had to do was send her son to get the full quantity.

The next morning she called her son and said to him: "Bring your flute, we are going to the farm."

There was no work for them to do in the farm but they hung around until sunset. Then she said: "Let us go home." The boy picked up his flute but his mother hit him on the head. "Foolish boy," she said, "don't you know how to forget your flute?"

So the boy left his flute behind. They passed seven streams and seven wilds and finally reached their home.

[97]

"Now you go back for your flute!"

The boy cried and protested but his mother pushed him out and told him that the hut would not contain both of them until he had gone back to the farm and brought gifts from the spirits.

The boy passed the seven streams and the seven wilds and came to the place where the spirits were bent in work.

"Mpf! mpf!" sniffed the boy in disgust. "I choke with the stench of spirits!"

The king of the spirits asked him what he came for.

"My mother sent me to get my flute. Mpf! mpf!"

"Will you recognize the flute if you see it?"

"What sort of question is that?" said the boy. "Who will not recognize his flute if he sees it? Mpf! mpf!"

The spirit then showed him a flute shining like yellow metal and the boy immediately said it was his.

"Take it and blow for us," said the spirit.

"I hope you have not been spitting into it," said the boy, wiping its mouth against his flank. Then he blew this song:

> King of Spirits he stinks
> Mpf mpf
> Old Spirit he stinks
> Mpf mpf
> Young Spirit he stinks
> Mpf mpf
> Mother Spirit she stinks
> Mpf mpf
> Father Spirit he stinks
> Mpf mpf

When he finished all the spirits were silent. Then their leader brought out two pots, one big and one small. Before the word was out of his mouth the boy had pounced on the big one.

"When you reach home call your mother and your father and break it before them. On your way if you hear *dum-dum*, run into the bush and if you hear *jam-jam* come out again."

Without stopping to thank the spirits the boy carried the pot and went away. He came to a certain place and heard *dum-dum*; he stayed on the road looking this way and that to see what it was. Then he heard *jam-jam* and went into the bush.

He passed the seven streams and seven wilds and reached home in the end. His mother who had been waiting for him outside their hut was happy when she saw the size of the pot.

[98]

"They said I should break it before my father and yourself,"
said the boy.

"What has your father got to do with it? Did he send you?"

She took the pot into her hut and shut the door. Then she filled
in every crack in the wall so that nothing might escape to her husband's junior wife. When everything was ready she broke the pot.
Leprosy, smallpox, yaws and worse diseases without names and
every abomination filled the hut and killed the woman and all her
children.

In the morning, as there was no sign of life in her hut, her husband pushed open the door, and peeped in. That peep was more
than enough. He struggled with the things fighting to come out
and eventually succeeded in shutting the door again. But by then
a few of the diseases and abominations had escaped and spread in
the world. But fortunately the worst of them—those without a
name—remained in that hut. (pp. 235–39)

This story, which many will recognize as a variant of the
widespread "Tale of the Kind and the Unkind Girls"[7] (#480
in the Aarne-Thompson tale type index), does not appear to
have much relevance to Ezeulu's tragedy until we examine its
morphology and placement within the novel. It will be recalled
that the tale is introduced at the time Ezeulu is pondering
whether to punish or forgive his people for failing to respond
adequately to his imprisonment. After the tale is told, Ezeulu
begins once again "to probe with the sensitiveness of a snail's
horns the possibility of reconciliation or, if that was too much,
of narrowing down the area of conflict." (p. 240) But while he
is considering the various alternatives before him, he suddenly
hears the voice of his god:

"Ta! Nwanu!" barked Ulu in his ear, as a spirit would in the ear
of an impertinent human child. "Who told you that this was your
own fight? . . . I say who told you that this was your own fight
which you could arrange to suit you? You want to save your friends
who brought you palm wine he-he-he-he-he! . . . Beware you do
not come between me and my victim or you may receive blows
not meant for you!" (pp. 240–41)

After this, Ezeulu is no longer uncertain about his course of
action. He views himself as "an arrow in the bow of his god,"

[99]

(p. 241) a vehicle of divine retribution for the waywardness of his people. Even the most influential elders of his clan cannot persuade him to change his mind about delaying the yam harvest. His people begin to suffer great hardships and deprivation, but he holds firm to this decision. It is only after one of his own sons dies, partly as a consequence of his vindictive obstinacy, that Ezeulu cracks under the strain and goes irretrievably mad. But by then the social and religious damage has been done. His people, to avoid starvation, have started taking offerings to the god of the Christians, who is said to have power to protect his followers from the anger of Ulu, Ezeulu's god, and thereafter most of the yams that are harvested in the village are harvested in the name of this new god. Ezeulu's perverse leadership thus results in the destruction of the very traditions that he, as chief priest, was supposed to defend and perpetuate.

The structural and thematic parallels between Ezeulu's story and our folktale may now be drawn more explicitly. In both narratives proper conduct is rewarded and improper conduct punished. The boy in the folktale who obeys the spirits of the yam-field and always tells the truth receives a pot "filled with every good thing"; his half brother who disobeys and insults the spirits is given a pot containing horrible "diseases and abominations" which quickly kill him and his closest relatives. Similarly, Ezeulu prospers as a chief priest as long as he subordinates himself to Ulu, but he brings ruin upon himself and his kinsmen when he commits the unforgivable sin of interpreting his own will as his god's. The contrast provided by the binary repetition of opposite events in the folktale finds expression in the novel in the antithetical actions preceding and following Ezeulu's decision to upset the agricultural calendar—e.g., his performance and later non-performance of the required rituals. It is therefore of utmost significance that the folktale is told at the precise moment that Ezeulu is trying to decide how to deal with people and that immediately after the recitation of the tale Ezeulu imagines he hears Ulu bark in his ear and tell him which course to take. The tale was no doubt deliberately inserted at this pivotal point in the novel as a commentary on previous and subsequent events, for it functions admirably as a paradigm of the entire novel, summarizing in schematic form the most relevant past action and foreshadowing the eventual downfall of the hero. Achebe could not have chosen a more appropriate tale to distil his message.

Additional proof that Achebe intended the tale as a gloss on Ezeulu's behavior can be found in at least two places. The action in the tale itself occurs on a farm which "was at the boundary between the land of men and the land of spirits," and it is human and spiritual interaction there that yields productive and then disastrous results. The most significant action in the novel takes place in the mind of Ezeulu, who as priest of Ulu is believed to be "half-man, half-spirit." At first his human and spiritual parts are in happy equilibrium, but later they come into conflict, ultimately tearing him apart. The analogy between the farm as demiworld and Ezeulu as demigod must have been obvious to Achebe.

There is also some evidence to suggest that Achebe, in his subtle way, may have been trying to alert the reader to make the connection between the folktale and Ezeulu's story. When Ezeulu receives the news that he is to be released from prison, he tells one of his kinsmen that he now intends to return home "to wrestle with my own people whose hand I know and who know my hand. I am going home to challenge all those who have been poking their fingers into my face to come outside their gate and meet me in combat and whoever throws the other will strip him of his anklet." (p. 221) His kinsman excitedly compares this to "the challenge of Eneke Ntulukpa to man, bird and beast" and breaks into "the taunting song with which the bird, Eneke once challenged the whole world." (p. 221) One doesn't know from reading the novel if this bird is at all related to the oft-mentioned proverbial "little bird, nza, who ate and drank and challenged his personal god to single combat,"[10] but even if it isn't, the image of Ezeulu as an over-ambitious wrestler[11] is established quite firmly in the reader's mind by Achebe's direct comparison of the old priest to Eneke Ntulukpa. The next time we hear of this world-challenging bird is just before the folktale is told. Ezeulu's children Nwafo and Obiageli are arguing over which tale their mother should tell. Obiageli suggests the tale of Onwuero, the beautiful maiden who married a fish.[12] Nwafo objects that "we have heard it too often" and is about to suggest another when Obiageli cuts in, saying, "All right. Tell us about Eneke Ntulukpa." (p. 235) The mother, having "searched her memory for a while and found what she looked for," then proceeds to tell the tale quoted above. This is obviously not the tale of Eneke Ntulukpa, since it has nothing to do with a world-challenging bird, but rather, as demonstrated earlier, it is a paradigmatically symbolic redaction of the career of Ezeulu, whose name has already been inextricably linked to that of the bird. It is as if Achebe, eager for us to see the submerged parallels between the folktale and the novel, felt he had to hint, at least obliquely, that the tale had something to do with his priest-hero. This he did by making it appear that the mother was about to tell the story of Eneke Ntulukpa, a code name for Ezeulu. Indeed, the name of the bird stands almost as a title to the tale, forcing us to recognize the connection.

Achebe's sensitive handling of this tale in *Arrow of God* suggests that his art is far more subtle and sophisticated than it appears on the surface. And to this it should be added that some of his techniques seem to be more African than European. For example, his ability to utilize folktales as relevant social commentary in symbolic form is surely something he acquired at home, not abroad. Léopold Senghor once said, "The traditional African narrative is woven out of everyday events. In this it is a question neither of anecdotes nor of things 'taken from life.' All the events become images, and so acquire paradigmatic value and point beyond the moment."[13] Achebe, perhaps because he is a consummate *African* artist, transforms even seemingly trivial events in his novels into meaningful imagistic paradigms which point well beyond the moment.

NOTES

1 See, e.g., the reviews of *Arrow of God* by Phoebe Adams, *Atlantic Monthly*, 220 (December 1967), 150, and I. N. C. Aniebo, *Nigeria Magazine*, No. 81 (June 1964), p. 150.
2 Review of *Arrow of God* by Ronald Christ, *New York Times Book Review*, December 17, 1967, p. 22.
3 Review by D. J. Enright, *New Statesman*, April 3, 1964, p. 531.
4 Robert Plant Armstrong, "The Characteristics and Comprehension of a National Literature—Nigeria," *Proceedings of a Conference on African Languages and Literatures Held at Northwestern University, April 28–30, 1966*, ed. Jack Berry *et al.* (n.p., n.d.), p. 123.
5 For discussion of his use of proverbs in fiction, see my "The Palm-Oil with Which Achebe's Words Are Eaten," *African Literature Today*, No. 1 (1968), pp. 3–18, reprinted in the preceding chapter, and Austin Shelton, "The 'Palm-Oil' of Language: Proverbs in Chinua Achebe's Novels," *Modern Language Quarterly*, 30, No. 1 (1969), 86–111. For discussion of his use of folktales in his novels, see Donald Weinstock and Cathy Ramadan, "Symbolic Structure in *Things Fall Apart*," *Critique*, 11 (1968–69), 33–41, and John O. Jordan, "Culture Conflict and Social Change in Achebe's *Arrow of God*," *Critique*, 13 (1971), 66–82.
6 All quotations are taken from Chinua Achebe's *Arrow of God* (London, 1964).
7 For a thorough historical-geographical study of this tale, see Warren E. Roberts, *The Tale of the Kind and the Unkind Girls: Aa-Th 480 and Related Tales* (Berlin, 1958).
8 Antti Aarne and Stith Thompson, *The Types of the Folktale: A Classification and Bibliography* (Helsinki, 1964).
9 I have not been able to find texts of this tale in published collections of Ibo folktales, but tales about a man or bird who defeats everyone in wrestling except his own *chi* (personal god) are quite common. See, e.g., Rems Nna Umeasiegbu, *The Way We Lived: Ibo Customs and Stories* (London, 1969), pp. 136–37, and Cyprian Ekwensi, *The Great Elephant Bird* (London, 1965), pp. 28–30. Achebe himself includes such a tale in *Arrow of God*, pp. 31–32.

Austin Shelton, in his article on Achebe's proverbs cited above, makes the following observation on Eneke Ntulukpa:

> "The meaning here is not immediately apparent, but depends upon a juxtaposition of opposites: *énéké* is an obnoxious, inedible black spiny grasshopper, whereas *ńtūlūkpà* is a very tasty herb. Thus placing the two together creates a challenge to all people, who hate one and love the other. Nwodika's remark thus takes on an ironic tone, and can be applied to Ezeulu, who is represented as a priest of a powerful god, but widely disliked as a cantankerous person. In such a match as

that proposed by Ezeulu, opponents would be happy to fight Ezeulu as a person, but would fear him as the agent of the god." (pp. 101–02)

10 This proverb is frequently used by Achebe. In *Arrow of God* it appears on page 17, in *Things Fall Apart* on page 26, and in *No Longer at Ease* on page 163.

11 For a discussion of the wrestler image in one of Achebe's earlier novels, see the preceding chapter. Eldred Jones also mentions this image in his review of *Arrow of God* in *The Journal of Commonwealth Literature*, No. 1 (September 1965), p. 176.

12 A version of this tale can be found in Ekwensi, *Great Elephant Bird*, pp. 3–4.

13 Quoted in Janheinz Jahn, *Muntu* (London, 1961), p. 211.

WOLE SOYINKA AND THE
HORSES OF SPEECH

The Yoruba have a saying that "proverbs are the horses of speech; if communication is lost, we use proverbs to find it."[1] In actual practice, of course, the Yoruba, like any other people, command a whole stable of gnomic horses and groom them to serve a variety of rhetorical purposes. They can be employed not only to retrieve communication gone astray but to speed it up, slow it down, convey weighty messages, deliver lighthearted jests, sharpen arguments, blunt criticism, clarify difficult ideas and disguise simple ones beyond easy recognition. The same proverb, in fact, can be an ordinary beast of burden or a rare racing thoroughbred, depending on its use—and user. The real master of proverbs is one who is able to summon the entire cavalry at will and make them spontaneously perform precisely those tricks he has in mind. To do this, he must be in complete control of their movements at all times, harnessing their versatile energies with such skill that they cannot bolt off in directions he did not intend. He must be an expert wrangler with words.

Wole Soyinka is one of these. No other African writer—except possibly Chinua Achebe or D. O. Fagunwa—has displayed so much agility in manipulating traditional verbal formulae. Of course, Achebe and Fagunwa write prose fiction, a pliant kind of literature which affords them the opportunity to insert proverbs into narration as well as dialogue. Soyinka, writing as a dramatist, must put all his words into the mouths of his characters; he can never speak in his own voice or in the guise of an omniscient chronicler. Yet even this formal limitation does not prevent him from getting more literary mileage out of African oral art than any other writer on the continent. Indeed, the limitation may actually work to his advantage, since it forces him to employ proverbs and other forms of fixed-phrase folklore in situations where they are dramatically appropriate, situations of dynamic human interaction in which formulaic sayings are expected to have some influence on the course of subsequent events. Soyinka returns folklore to the folk, and in so doing, enriches his theatrical art immeasurably.

Take characterization, for example. The personalities of Soyinka's characters are often very clearly defined by the proverbs they use. In *A Dance of the Forests*[2] it is not difficult to determine that Agboreko, ironically called the "Elder of Sealed Lips," is a garrulous old windbag. Every time he opens his mouth ponderous proverbs tumble out, followed by tag lines such as "Proverb to bones and silence" or "Oracle to living and silence," which identify them as words of traditional wisdom. The trouble with Agboreko's sayings is that they contribute little or nothing to any conversation he enters because they bear only the most oblique relation to the matters under discussion. He appears to be citing proverbs merely for the sake of impressing others with his erudition, not for the sake of improving communication. To Agboreko, conventional form is obviously much more important than significant content. When advising an Old Man to be patient, he unreels a string of ancient adages, only a few of which seem relevant to the message he wishes to convey:

> "The eye that looks downwards will certainly see the nose. The hand that dips to the bottom of the pot will eat the biggest snail. The sky grows no grass but if the earth called her barren, it will drink no more milk. The foot of the snake is not split in two like a man's or in hundreds like a centipede's, but if Agere could dance patiently like the snake, he would uncoil the chain that leads into the dead. . . ." (p. 38)

This is colorful language but little else. The proverbs are not without overtones of applicable meaning, but their primary function is to display Agboreko's flair for dredging up miscellaneous tidbits of prefabricated wisdom. The situation may have called for the recitation of a few pithy proverbs, but offering them in such dense profusion seems a classic example of pseudo-intellectual overkill. Agboreko is plainly a pedantic fool.

Makuri, the old barber in *The Swamp Dwellers*, is a very different kind of person. Humble, content with his meagre lot in life and obedient to his gods, he does not quote proverbs in an effort to prove himself superior to others. He quotes them only when they might serve to soothe someone in a state of emotional discomfort. In his long discussions with the blind beggar he resorts to proverbs three times: once to persuade the beggar, who has become irritated by his pointed questions, to remain with him, twice to comment sympathetically on the beggar's unhappy past experiences. The proverbs he uses ("The blind man does not hurry for fear he out-walks his guide"; "Every god shakes a beggar by the hand"; "The hands of the gods are unequal")[3] reflect his conviction that men, while dependent upon one another, are ultimately at the mercy of unpredictable gods. The proverbs also illustrate that even a deeply religious person like Makuri may find it necessary to adopt a fatalistic attitude toward human existence in order to cope with the harsh uncertainties of life in the swamps. For despite his stubborn show of faith in men and gods, Makuri is a resigned pessimist at heart.

The blind beggar, on the other hand, has great hopes for the future. Though he has been exposed to the cruelties of nature and his fellow man, he believes the world can be changed for the better. He plans to spend the rest of his life sowing seeds of renewal in fertile lands he has reclaimed from the swamps. The beggar's optimism is apparent in the proverbs he cites when trying to persuade Igwezu to return to the swamps to join in the good work:

> "The swallows find their nest again when the cold is over. Even the bats desert dark holes in the trees and flap wet leaves with wings of leather. There were wings everywhere as I wiped my feet against your threshold. I heard the cricket scratch himself beneath the armpit as the old man said to me. . . ." (pp. 41–42)

All the imagery suggests that the season has changed, that the time is now becoming ripe for the kind of revolution that the beggar envisions for human society. The proverbs define the beggar's attitude toward the new world to which he has totally committed himself.

If Soyinka's proverbs functioned only as agents of character-ization or as cheap dabs of local color, they would be no more remarkable than the proverbs in plays by many of his less talented contemporaries. However, Soyinka frequently weaves them so intricately into the fabric of dramatic action that they become a vital part of the total artistic design, a part which could not be altered or eliminated without destroying the com-plex patterns of human interaction upon which the drama itself depends. In other words, they are not meaningless, exotic decorations but elements central to the intense theatrical experi-ence Soyinka attempts to create. An examination of their dramatic function in three comic plays will reveal the skill with which Soyinka exploits their esthetic possibilities.

Perhaps it would be best to begin with *The Trials of Brother Jero*, a play which contains only one proverb. Why should this play be so empty of proverbs while others are so full? One answer may lie in the nature of the comedy itself, another in Soyinka's strategy of dramatic presentation. *The Trials of Brother Jero* is a farce with a religious charlatan as hero; it begins with Brother Jero revealing to the audience that he makes his living by pretending to be a prophet. He then offers to show us "one rather eventful day" in his life when his deceitful proph-eteering was almost brought to a catastrophic end. Thus, right from the start, we are made aware not only of Jero's duplicity but also of his ultimate survival as a rogue-hero, and this enables us to sit back without qualms of conscience and enjoy the precarious maneuvers he employs to maintain his false position. The play turns into a parade of hilarious picaresque adventures, with Jero occasionally stepping outside the action to comment on the brilliance of his strategems or the follies of his followers. Jero's schizoid role is crucial to the comedy, for as both actor and observer in the drama, he fluctuates freely between total involvement and total detachment. He is a player who wears more than one mask, and much of our delight comes from seeing him switch them so swiftly and speak so honestly about his dishonesty. He is a human paradox.

Farce, of course, is not a subtle medium, so its capacity to exploit paradox is rather limited. Farce demands sharp outlines —nothing ambiguous, everything clear, blunt, direct. The audience must be able to follow the thread of dramatic discourse without getting tangled in hidden nuances of meaning or led astray by loose ends of tangential thought. In Soyinka's play, it is "Articulate Jero," our talkative host, who sees to it that no one loses the central thread. He may be a paradox, but he is a very transparent one who does not in any way obscure our vision of essential matters. In fact, through him we see things more clearly than we otherwise would. He magnifies rather than diminishes our insights into human nature.

Perhaps this is one reason he does not ordinarily speak in proverbs. If his thoughts were clothed in picturesque metaphors and symbols, he might be unable to communicate with such lucidity. Worse yet, he might run the risk of being misunderstood, and this would seriously undermine our confidence in him as an honest trickster. His role as master of ceremonies in the farce demands that he be completely frank and forthright, never deviously indirect.

The one proverb Jero quotes is therefore extremely significant. It appears at the beginning of his opening monologue, when he is detailing the different kinds of prophets one finds in the world. "There are eggs," he says, "and there are eggs,"[4] the implication being that though they all look exactly alike on the surface, some will be good and others rotten. "Same thing with prophets," he declares, forcing us to recognize the ubiquity of apostasy and religious hypocrisy even in the saintliest of holy occupations. As he continues speaking, however, it soon becomes plain that he himself is a professional imposter, one who relishes duping the gullible by posing as a beach evangelist blessed with a divine gift of fortunetelling. His proverb serves not only to alert us to the possibility that he might be a bad egg but also to introduce the theme of duplicity which comes to dominate the entire play. It proves a very prophetic proverb.

In *The Lion and the Jewel*[5] Soyinka makes use of a similar theme but adopts a different strategy of comic presentation. The play recounts how wily old Baroka, through a clever ruse, succeeds in seducing young Sidi, a conceited village girl who has refused to marry him. The comic thrust is once again provided by an elaborate act of deception, but the audience is not made aware of the subtlety of Baroka's maneuvers until the very end. Surprise is an important element in the play. Because Baroka is not a transparent trickster, we cannot predict how or even whether he will manage to win the "jewel." His climactic treachery is therefore almost as delightfully astonishing to us as it is to Sidi.

The proverbs in the play help to define the nature of the dramatic conflict as a battle of the sexes. Most of them can be found in the seduction scene, where they serve both parties as ammunition, Sidi playfully firing them as taunts at Baroka for his supposed impotence, Baroka answering with a barrage of well-placed barbs by which he bullies and eventually corners his prey. It is evident that Baroka also knows how to use gentler means of persuasion, for once he has cornered Sidi, he turns on his verbal charm and overwhelms her with wise-sounding apothegms pregnant with erotic imagery. Indeed, the entire scene is a study in the art of rhetoric, for Baroka achieves his purpose primarily through the skillful selection and manipulation of accepted truths. He constructs an argument in aphorisms, clinching his points with pertinent proverbs.

One brief illustration will suffice. When Baroka shows Sidi thestamp-making machine in his bedroom and says he wants to put her image on the first stamps to be printed in Ilujinle, Sidi is struck speechless. The stage directions say she "drowns herself totally in the contemplation" of this idea. Baroka, meanwhile, talks on, first in simple, straightforward language, then in elaborate metaphors. Aware that she is only half listening, he indulges in double talk, occasionally pausing to ask her questions:

> "Among the bridges and the murderous roads,
> Below the humming birds which
> Smoke the face of Sango, dispenser of
> The snake-tongue lightning; between this moment
> And the reckless broom that will be wielded
> In these years to come, we must leave
> Virgin plots of lives, rich decay
> And the tang of vapour rising from
> Forgotten heaps of compost, lying
> Undisturbed . . . But the skin of progress
> Masks, unknown, the spotted wolf of sameness . . .
> Does sameness not revolt your being,
> My daughter?" (p. 52)

By this time Sidi "is only capable of a bewildered nod," and Baroka, having seated himself beside her on the bed, resumes his mystifying patter. Soon Sidi is feebly protesting, "I can no longer see the meaning, Baroka . . . words are like beetles/ Boring at my ears, and my head/ Becomes a jumping bean." Baroka then closes in for the kill, bombarding her with old saws cleverly honed to make a single voluptuous point:

> "The proof of wisdom is the wish to learn
> Even from children. And the haste of youth
> Must learn its temper from the gloss
> Of ancient leather, from a strength
> Knit close along the grain . . .
> The old must flow into the new, Sidi,
> Not blind itself or stand foolishly
> Apart. A girl like you must inherit
> Miracles which age alone reveals.
> Is this not so?" (pp. 53–54)

Sidi, completely under his spell, replies, "Everything you say, Bale,/ Seems wise to me." Baroka immediately pours out another aphrodisiac analogy:

> "Yesterday's wine alone is strong and blooded, child,
> And though the Christians' holy book denies
> The truth of this, old wine thrives best

Within a new bottle. The coarseness
Is mellowed down, and the rugged wine
Acquires a full and rounded body." (p. 54)

By now Sidi is "quite overcome," but Soyinka cannot resist letting Baroka conclude the scene with a singularly appropriate image of another sort:

"Those who know little of Baroka think
His life one pleasure-living course.
But the monkey sweats, my child,
The monkey sweats,
It is only the hair upon his back
Which still deceives the world." (p. 54)

The proverbs in this scene are working brilliantly at several different levels simultaneously. They are being used to befuddle Sidi, to spell out graphically Baroka's erotic intentions, and to keep the audience amused and alert to what is going on. We understand every double-entendre in the colorful pronouncements that Sidi, in her confusion, finds "wise," for Baroka is communicating with us in a decipherable code even while impressing Sidi by appearing to speak in unfathomable riddles. Soyinka moves easily from one level to another, juggling meaning and meaninglessness with dazzling dexterity.

But that is not all. As authentic bits of native gnomic lore, the proverbs are also functioning autonomously as independent statements about the nature of human wisdom, the deceptiveness of outward appearances, the complementary interaction of opposites—age and youth, male and female, tradition and change, etc. Yet every one of these statements is of relevance to the drama and is therefore contributing something of its own to the network of meaning in the play. They are individual resonators of important themes, electric transmitters of germinal ideas. Proverbs function in all these ways in *The Lion and the Jewel* because Soyinka knows how to take advantage of the opportunities afforded by their very nature as vehicles of indirect communication.

Kongi's Harvest[6] is Soyinka's most proverb-riddled play, and it is probably significant that it deals with African politics. Perhaps nothing straight can be said in a world so crooked. Perhaps indirection and equivocation are essential for survival. One must either learn to speak in ambiguous conundrums or lose the privilege of speaking at all. This appears to be the only choice—unless, of course, one is at the very top of the pyramid of power. Kongi never speaks in proverbs. He simply doesn't find it necessary or expedient to do so, for as an enlightened modern despot, he knows that there is no one left outside prison walls for him to fear or placate. He knows, too, that if worse were to come to worse, he has at his command means of persuasion more powerful than mere words. So there is no reason for him to resort to circuitous speech; he can afford to be direct.

He also happens to be opposed to all things traditional, for he intends to modernize his state completely, even to the point of reforming the language of government. Early in the play one of his ghost writers reminds another that "the period of isolated saws and wisdoms is over, superseded by a more systematic formulation of comprehensive philosophies." (p. 24) To Kongi then, proverbs are not just unnecessary; they are downright passé and potentially destructive of the ideals of the modern nation-state. He doesn't want anyone to use them.

To squelch traditionalism and enshrine himself in power, Kongi plans an impressive formal inaugural ceremony. It is to take the form of a ritualized festival,[7] the highlight of which will be the moment that Oba Danlola, a traditional ruler, presents Kongi with the New Yam, an act symbolizing Danlola's spiritual submission to the new regime. Danlola, of course, is currently under preventive detention. There's the rub. How does one persuade a political enemy to participate in a phony ritual designed to rob him forever of power? Kongi's answer is to offer him a small bribe—the promise of a reprieve for a group of political prisoners awaiting execution. All this is done in the clearest clinical language.

Danlola's response to any gesture made by Kongi or his followers is to babble in proverbs. In fact, in the first scene Danlola is revealed to be living in a state of near verbal anarchy. He is technically in a detention camp, but he and his retinue are singing, dancing, drumming and carrying on like frenzied performers in a folk opera. When the Superintendent attempts to intervene and stop their fun, Danlola quickly puts him down with a string of proverbs. His words and subsequent threats are so intimidating that the Superintendent is soon apologizing profusely in Danlola's own idiom—proverbs:

"I am only the fowl droppings that stuck to your slippers when you strolled in the back yard. The child is nothing; it is only the glory of his forebears that the world sees and tolerates in him." (p. 6)

Danlola has forced him to change his language and sing to a different tune.

Danlola has no intention of obediently participating in Kongi's festival but his words and actions are designed to give the impression that he will do as he has been told. His task is to deceive the deceiver. This he does by pretending to get ready for the festival, pretending he will take part, and pretending he knows nothing about a revolt planned by Segi and Daodu. To conceal his true feelings yet still speak the truth, he normally hides behind equivocations couched in proverbs. A number of his sayings reflect his preoccupation with disguise:

"The ostrich also sports plumes but
I've yet to see that wise bird
Leave the ground." (p. 48)

"When a dog hides a bone does he not
Throw up sand?" (p. 48)

"Only a phony drapes himself in deeper indigo
Than the son of the deceased." (p. 64)

Danlola and Kongi's other enemies eventually succeed in spoiling the festival and cursing its chief celebrant. It has been a contest between Might and Cunning, with Cunning winning because he knows how to work by indirection. It has also been a struggle between Old and New, Ornate and Plain, Tradition and

Modernity. The side with the greatest maneuverability always seems to triumph.

Soyinka's proverbs are capable of carrying us to the heart of his drama. By studying how they function and what they mean in a play, we can gain not only a better understanding of his intentions but also a deeper appreciation of his art and craft as a playwright. Soyinka's plays reward this kind of study, for if proverbs are truly "horses of speech," Soyinka is undoubtedly one of Africa's greatest verbal equestrians.

NOTES

1 This proverb was collected in 1968 from Oyekan Owomoyela, a Yoruba doctoral candidate in theatre arts at the University of California at Los Angeles. Printed versions can be found in Charlotte and Wolf Leslau, *African Proverbs* (Mount Vernon, 1962), p. 5, and Isaac O. Delano, *Owe L'Esin Oro: Yoruba Proverbs —Their Meaning and Usage* (Ibadan, 1966), pp. v, ix, 109.
2 Wole Soyinka, *A Dance of the Forests* (London, 1963). All quotations are taken from this edition.
3 Wole Soyinka, *Three Short Plays* (London, 1969), pp. 14, 15, 26. All quotations are taken from this edition.
4 *Ibid.*, p. 45.
5 Wole Soyinka, *The Lion and the Jewel* (London, 1963). All quotations are taken from this edition.
6 Wole Soyinka, *Kongi's Harvest* (London, 1967). All quotations are taken from this edition.
7 Soyinka's debt to traditional Yoruba festivals in this and other plays is discussed by Oyin Ogunba in "The Traditional Content of the Plays of Wole Soyinka," *African Literature Today*, No. 4 (1970), pp. 2–18; No. 5 (1971), pp. 106–15.

CYPRIAN EKWENSI:
AN AFRICAN POPULAR NOVELIST

Of all the Africans who have written full-length novels in English, Cyprian Ekwensi perhaps best illustrates the dictum that practice does not make a writer perfect. At least nine novels (four of them still unpublished), six novelettes for schoolchildren, two collections of folktales, and dozens of short stories have poured from his pen, but not one is entirely free of amateurish blots and blunders, not one could be called the handiwork of a careful, skilled craftsman. Ekwensi may be simply too impatient an artist to take pains with his work or to learn by a calm, rational process of trial and error. When he is not repeating his old mistakes, he is stumbling upon spectacular new ones. As a consequence, many of his stories and novels can serve as excellent examples of how not to write fiction.

Part of his problem is that he attempts to write truly popular literature. Unlike other African writers who address themselves to Europe or to an educated African elite, Ekwensi prides himself on being a writer for the masses, a writer who can communicate with any African literate in English. He does not pretend to be profound, subtle or erudite; he would rather be considered entertaining, exciting, sensational. His ambition is to produce thrillers like those that first stimulated his interest in reading and writing. Unfortunately, he seems to have obtained most of his stimulation from third-rate American movies and fourth-rate British and American paperback novels, for these are certainly the most pronounced influences on what he has written. In his favor it may be said that Ekwensi possesses a peculiar talent for imitating bad models well and adapting them to fit into an African setting. He is in this respect an accomplished literary *assimilado*. If his fiction still retains a few vestigial Africanisms, they tend to be all but obliterated under a smooth veneer of slick Western varnish. Nevertheless, these immanent Africanisms should not be overlooked in any evaluation of his writing, for they help to explain some of his idiosyncrasies. This essay will explore Ekwensi's debts to Western popular literature traditions and to indigenous oral traditions and will assess the effects of such influences on his fiction.

Ekwensi's first borrowings were from fairly harmless sources. As a young schoolboy he had been thrilled by his reading of simplified editions of English popular novels: "I was reading Rider Haggard, Edgar Wallace, Dickens, Sapper, Bates. At Government College in Ibadan we could recite whole chunks of *King Solomon's Mines. Nada the Lily* was a favourite; so was *She*, and *Allan Quatermain . . . Treasure Island* [was] unforgettable."[1] The impact that these juvenile classics made on Ekwensi can be discerned in one of his first attempts at long fiction, *Juju Rock*,[2] which reverberates with echoes from *Treasure Island* and *King Solomon's Mines*. The story is narrated by its hero, Rikku, a young Fulani schoolboy in western Nigeria who serves as a guide to three Englishmen on an expedition to mysterious Juju Rock in the northern grasslands. The men are searching for a lost goldmine and for an old sailor who had disappeared on an earlier expedition and was thought to have located the mine. As they near their destination, Rikku, like Jim Hawkins, overhears his companions plotting to kill him as soon as the gold is found. Rikku escapes, disguises himself as a canoe boy, and bravely rejoins the evil three.

When the group arrives at Juju Rock, Robert Louis Stevenson gives way to Rider Haggard. Rikku and his companions come upon a dangerous tribal "Secret Society" carrying out its rituals, and a fierce battle in a dark cave ensues. The tribesmen overcome Rikku and the three Englishmen and are preparing to sacrifice them when an unexpected rescue party arrives and saves them. Rikku then finds the old sailor in the cave and after a few more scuffles and narrow escapes, hears him tell his side of the story. Thus, as in most school readers narrated in the first

person, loose ends are conveniently tied off and mysteries effi-
ciently explained so events can be rapidly concluded. As might
be expected, the three villains end up in prison and Rikku returns to school a national hero.

If any further proof is required to demonstrate that *Juju Rock*
was written in imitation of juvenile adventure fiction, it can be
found in the text itself, for Ekwensi, in his eagerness to place his
story in this genre, drew very specific parallels for his readers.
The first chapter begins as follows:

> Now that I have been through it all, and the whole thing seems so
> distant and remote, I sometimes wonder what it was that lured
> me into that JUJU ROCK adventure. Boyish curiosity, perhaps;
> an eagerness to learn more, and the influence of "Wild West"
> fiction and very recent reading of "King Solomon's Mines." In
> many ways JUJU ROCK was like something out of those
> romantic days. [3]

Having made this point, Ekwensi apparently did not want anyone to forget it. Later in the story, when Rikku has been captured by the "Secret Society" and fears he is about to be speared
to death by the Chief Priest, Ekwensi has him say:

> I could see the eyes of the Chief Priest as he glared at me and I
> knew he hated me with all his might. This was certainly the end.
> Never again would I have the joy of reading Wild West stories, or
> books like "King Solomon's Mines." [4]

The chapter in which this occurs, it should be noted, is entitled
"Showdown at Juju Rock." Ekwensi was doing everything he
could to ensure that readers would associate his novelette with
the "thrillers" or "real life adventure stories" that boys enjoyed
reading at school.

Ekwensi's familiarity with "Wild West" stories is most clearly
displayed in *The Passport of Mallam Ilia*, another of his early
attempts at juvenile adventure fiction set in the cattle lands of
northern Nigeria. Here is a scene borrowed lock, stock and
barrel from stagecoach melodramas of the American Southwest:

> Mallam Usuman quickly guided his horse up the bank of the
> stream, and, riding slowly along, studied the transport for a time.

Experience told him that they had been travelling for some time and were therefore very tired. He dug his heels into the flanks of his horse. In a moment he had drawn up beside them and levelled his gun.

"Whoever you are," he snarled, "you can choose."

The transport stopped and the driver turned his sun-scorched face towards him. There was anger in his flaming eyes.

"Which do you choose," Usuman went on, "your life or your money?"

"There—there is no money," stammered the driver.

"Don't lie!'

Usuman with his quick eye had already seen the wooden box beneath the driver's seat; but now, as the passengers began to complain and show signs of terror, Usuman noticed that there was a woman in the carriage. She was sitting tightly wedged in between the other passengers, calm and cool. She lifted her black veil for a moment and Usuman's eyes widened at the sight of her face. She was beautiful.

The driver must have been watching him, for he said in Hausa: "You like her then? Unfortunately, she is not for you . . ."

"You rat!" snapped Usuman. "Throw down the money and drive on."

The driver glanced from the bore of the rifle into Usuman's face and decided to obey. He got down, fumbled for a moment, and was bringing out something from under the box when Usuman shot him in the hand and a British revolver dropped to the ground.

"Now will you put down the box?"

Cursing, the driver pushed down the box with his left hand and climbed back into his seat.

"Not yet," said Usuman. He turned and winked at the lady. "Open the carriage and let her step down!"[5]

Ekwensi was apparently familiar with all the standard clichés of the Western. Whether he picked them up from fiction or from films cannot be determined, but it is clear that he had no qualms about using them, even if it meant dressing Billy the Kid in the robes and turban of a Hausa Mallam.

Burning Grass, Ekwensi's first attempt at longer fiction,[6] also bears the imprint of the Western branding iron. There are cattle rustlings, stampedes, galloping horses, saloon confrontations, and ferocious battles galore. Here is an archetypal ambush:

Hodio's gallop out of New Chanka quickened as his temper mounted. He dug his heels hard into his horse's flanks, cursing the while, slashing cruelly down with his cane. Lying close to his horse's mane, his eyes darted keenly into every nook and crevice of the scrub . . .

His horse twisted and turned as it followed the crooked path before him. Shehu and his men had had too much of a start. At this rate, he might never catch up with them . . .

He slowed down. The large rock ahead of him would bear no prints. But something else seemed imminent. He could almost feel a third presence. He got down, climbed the large rock. From the top he commanded a grand view of the country behind him. It was a dead end, true enough. But somewhere behind this rock should be another path. It might take long to find, perhaps too long.

He decided to search. He turned. Like a flash, the arrows whizzed past his ear. He threw himself flat down. His horse broke away, yelping with pain. He could see the butts of at least three arrows in its flank. Slowly the horse would die of the poison in the iron tips.

He looked down the bottom of the rock and saw three men labouring up towards him. The biggest of them all was Shehu, the man he sought.[7]

What is most remarkable about these quoted excerpts is that they are very accurate imitations. Ekwensi had an uncommonly good ear for narrative style, a gift for mimicry, and a knack for transplanting un-African events onto African soil. He could make Nigerian schoolboys imagine an impossible treasure hunt or feel at home on the range because he had mastered the conventions and commonplaces of foreign juvenile adventure fiction and knew how to domesticate them. His was a literature of imitation and adaptation, not a literature of imagination and original invention. So long as he continued to address an adolescent audience, his fiction remained as innocuous and unobjectionable as the material upon which it was modelled. It was when he began to try to reach an older audience that he turned to less innocent models and descended from the highroads of classic juvenile literature to the more pedestrian paths of earthy popular fiction.

[120]

Ekwensi's first tentative step in this new direction was taken in 1947, when he published a forty-four-page pamphlet novel entitled *When Love Whispers*. This was one of the first inexpensive paperback novelettes, now commonly called chapbooks,[8] to be issued in Nigeria, and like so many of those that have followed since, it was essentially the story of a maiden in distress. Beautiful, pure-hearted Ashoka, whose fiancé has just left for engineering studies in England, finds herself in continual difficulty. She is kidnapped, almost sold to an odious white man in a neighboring French territory, and eventually seduced by her fiancé's best friend. Unable to abort her pregnancy, she marries a third man whom she doesn't love. The wages of sin are sorrow.

Appropriately enough, *When Love Whispers* is written in a style which closely approximates that found in much drugstore pulp magazine fiction. Ekwensi must have known this type of literature quite well, for he was able to echo it very faithfully. The following passage is taken from the first few pages of the novelette:

> She loved him. She had promised to marry him. She was waiting now, hoping and praying for that great day when both of them would stand before the priest and say those age-old words. . . . And then they would walk down arm in arm, she in her white bridal dress, he in his starched collar.[9]

It must be remembered that at this early stage in his literary career Ekwensi was accustomed to addressing his fiction to a young audience, so he had little experience in writing passionate love scenes. This may explain why love-making is described with such reticence in *When Love Whispers*. In later novels Ekwensi grew much bolder and seemed to relish going through all the motions of a seduction scene, but during his apprenticeship he didn't dare treat sex too explicitly. Here, for example, is how Ashoka loses her virginity:

> She turned her face towards him in the moonlight, and there were points of fire in his eyes.
> "You're just too beautiful for words," he said. "Is that not how the song goes?"

She said nothing.

She felt his hand on her cheeks, and then he was touching soft parts of her, and still she said nothing. Then his lips were hot on hers and she was sighing.

"Leave me!" she shouted suddenly, pushing him back. "Let me go: you thief! You thief! I—I shall never see you again."[10]

In Ekwensi's later novels there was never any doubt about what the thief had stolen or which soft parts he had touched.

Perhaps it was the enormous popular success of *When Love Whispers*[11] that prompted Ekwensi to write two full-length novels about the misadventures of liberated Nigerian women. *Jagua Nana*, probably his most successful work, records the ups and downs of an aging Lagos prostitute who is in love with her work. In describing her affairs Ekwensi sometimes cannot suppress a vulgar smirk:

> He was beginning to regard himself as the rightful lover, always jealous. She got around him by mothering him. She went over now and sat on his knee, rubbing her thinly clad hips into his thighs. She threw one arm over his shoulder, so that her left breast snuggled close to his lips. Presently she felt his thick, rough lips close on the nipple. "A dog with food in his mouth does not bark," went the proverb.[12]

In *Iska*, his most recent novel, another city girl falls into a life of sin and later comes to rue her misspent youth. Ekwensi again spices the narrative with racy details:

> He came over, gripping the body of her breasts. She did not resist. Instead she took off her clothes and stood revealed before him.
>
> He gazed at her with his eyes nearly coming off their sockets. There she was on offer, the flesh of black woman, pale and bleached by a thousand cosmetic creams, completely devastating.[13]

Because his sinful heroines usually come to bad ends, Ekwensi can be viewed as a serious moralist whose novels offer instruction in virtue by displaying the tragic consequences of vice. But it is always quite clear to the reader that he is far more interested in vice than in virtue and that he aims to titillate as well as teach.

As Ekwensi moved from romantic love to torrid sex he also developed an interest in crime. The hero of his first full-length novel, *People of the City*, was both a crime reporter and a part-time band leader, a man in an excellent position to observe both lowlife and highlife in a Nigerian metropolis. Here is a typical scene from this stereotypical novel:

> The phone rang. Sango went over.
> "*West African Sensation* . . ."
> "May I speak to the editor, please?" The voice was tinny, strained, very excited.
> Sango could feel the tension.
> "The editor is not here."
> "Any reporter there?"
> "Yes . . . who's speaking, please?"
> The office became silent. Over the wires, Sango could smell news. It always gave him a kick to smell news. Even Lajide and his debtor had frozen and were looking at him, listening intently. Sango felt proud to impress Lajide with his importance.
> "Never mind who I am. If you want something for your paper, come out to the Magamu Bush, and you'll get it."
> "Where are you speaking from? Hello . . . Hello . . . Hello! Oh! He's hung up."[14]

Ekwensi was obviously still operating under the influence of Hollywood and popular pulp fiction.

It was perhaps inevitable that Ekwensi should eventually try his hand at detective fiction. *Yaba Roundabout Murder*, a chapbook he published in Lagos in 1962, relates how a clever police inspector catches a murderer by pretending to make advances to the murderer's wife. Many of the standard ingredients of detective fiction—the anonymous telephone tip, the trail of clues, the interrogations, the newspaper headlines, the cool-headed police inspector—can be found here, the only novelty being the African setting in which they appear. What detective novel does not have a scene something like the following:

> Inspector John Faolu walked up to the door and knocked. But he found the door open. There was no one in the room. He pressed the switch. There was no light. His torchlight showed him that

there was a bulb in the ceiling, but apparently it had not been connected to the mains. The house was a new one.

The room was in disorder. There was every sign that the occupants had left in a great hurry. Clothes were carelessly strewn on the bed.

The books on the table had been disarranged, and beneath this was a box which though closed, had a number of clothes sticking out of it.

Faolu took in the scene with deep interest.[15]

This passage and others like it reveal that Ekwensi was familiar with the whodunit genre, knew its stock situations and clichés, and had not lost his flair for imitating bad models well.

Given Ekwensi's extraordinary susceptibility to influences from Western popular literature, what, if anything, could he possibly be said to owe to indigenous oral traditions? Can it be seriously suggested that there is something characteristically African or, more precisely, something characteristic of African oral narrative art in his fiction? The answer to this question is a tentative yes. There are at least two features of Ekwensi's novels and novelettes that resemble and perhaps derive from features of oral narrative art. Whether these are exclusively African characteristics is doubtful, but it seems more likely that Ekwensi assimilated them from traditional African narratives than from traditional European or American tales. In the late nineteen-forties and early fifties, when he was just getting started as a writer, he avidly collected and translated Ibo folktales, publishing them in local magazines and later in booklets designed for use in schools.[16] In 1947 he also collected a long traditional tale of vengeance from "an aged Hausa Mallam" who offered it as a story that "would keep [his] readers awake all night."[17] Ekwensi published this tale fifteen years later under the title *An African Night's Entertainment.* Thus it may be said that both early and late in his writing career Ekwensi demonstrated an active interest in African oral narratives.

One of the features that Ekwensi's fiction shares with African folktales is a tendency to moralize, a tendency to use action and character to illustrate a thesis or underscore a point. Ekwensi's

heroes and heroines sometimes seem like cardboard personifications of virtue or vice. They are more complex and better
individualized than folktale heroes, but they give the same
impression of having been created for a specific didactic purpose. They are like wooden puppets clumsily manipulated to
spell out a conventional message. Ekwensi does not ordinarily
state his moral explicitly at the end, as do many traditional
storytellers, but he gives the reader enough nudges and winks
along the way to make the moral known.

Good examples of Ekwensi's heavyhanded moralizing can be
found in one of his most recent novels, *Beautiful Feathers*, the title
of which is based on an Ibo proverb: "However famous a man
is outside, if he is not respected inside his own home he is like a
bird with *beautiful feathers*, wonderful on the outside but ordinary
within."[18] The hero of the novel is a pan-Africanist politician
who is just beginning to win a reputation and following when
his marriage starts to collapse. His neglected wife not only refuses to prepare his meals but spites him by brazenly taking a
lover. Ekwensi has his hero recognize the mordant irony of his
situation:

> *Solidarity, where does it begin? Here, in my own home? I am the leader of
> the Nigerian Movement for African and Malagasy Solidarity. Wilson
> Iyari, good looking, famous outside. At home I am nothing. I am like a fowl
> with beautiful feathers on the outside for all to see. When the feathers are
> removed the flesh and bones underneath are the same as for any other fowl.
> I am not really different from other men. In fact, if only they knew how I am
> spited in my own home they would despise me. They would never again
> listen to me talking about solidarity.*[19]

Throughout the novel Ekwensi plays upon the proverbial image
of the ordinary fowl with beautiful feathers by continuing to
contrast sharply Wilson's successful public life with his steadily
deteriorating home life. For example, there is a splendid scene
in which Wilson, while addressing a group of political leaders
in his home, sees his wife go out to meet her lover.

> As he mentioned the word "solidarity" Wilson saw the door of the
> bedroom open. His wife, resplendent, came out, passed through

the sitting-room, and before they could rise to greet her she was outside, leaving a bewitching trail of *Balmain*.[20]

The contrast between Wilson's public and private life is presented with graphic clarity here, but Ekwensi is not content to leave it at that. A few lines later he firmly underlines the message so no one will miss it.

> *She is going to meet her lover*, Wilson thought. *I talk about solidarity. There it is! My own family split. But how can Africa be united when such a small unit as my family is not united?*[21]

Such heavyhandedness ruins some of Ekwensi's best effects. Even the ending of the novel is spoiled by a lack of subtlety. After having Wilson retire from politics and reunite with his wife, Ekwensi concludes:

> They had truly come together now. It could be said of him that he was famous outside and that at home he had the backing of a family united by bonds of love. Wilson's beautiful feathers had ceased to be superficial and had become a substantial asset.[22]

Ekwensi simply cannot resist the temptation to tell his readers what the action signifies. Like a traditional storyteller, he frames his tale to illustrate a proverb.

Another feature that Ekwensi's fiction shares with many African oral narratives is a circular structure. To use Joseph Campbell's terms, the hero undergoes a sequence of adventures involving a departure, an initiation and a return.[23] In the end he is usually back where he started, older and wiser for his experiences and purged of all personal excesses. He has accomplished his tasks, liquidated his lacks,[24] and achieved a state of emotional equilibrium. Sometimes he completes his cycle of adventures by repudiating new Western ways and affirming old African values. He returns, in other words, to his African essence, to his roots, abandoning deviant foreign patterns. He is, in a sense, a modern African culture hero.

A few examples of Ekwensi's reliance on circular structures will suffice. In three of his juvenile novelettes—*Juju Rock*, *The Leopard's Claw*, and *The Drummer Boy*—a boy-hero rejects school

life, enters a corrupt adult world where he encounters and over-
comes evil, and then, having proven his courage and integrity,
turns eagerly to the very life he had earlier rejected. In *Beautiful
Feathers* the hero becomes embroiled in European-style politics
but quits in order to save his marriage. He decides his family
means more to him than fame, so he gives up his Westernized,
individualistic pursuit of personal glory. In *People of the City* a
young man leaves his village in the Eastern Greens for the
glamour and easy money of the big city, but after being exposed
to some of the city's ills, temptations and tragedies, he yearns
for a cleaner life and departs for the Gold Coast to make a fresh
start. In *Jagua Nana* a childless middle-aged woman leaves her
idyllic village, turns to a life of prostitution in the city, and then
returns home to bear an illegitimate child. Austin J. Shelton has
persuasively argued that her return to the village is "more than
a symbol of the rejection of westernization," that it is in fact an
act of "rebushing" or ontological recession, "showing that [her]
very Africanism, *despite her Europeanization*, militates against her
remaining permanently in the city where she has been separated
from all the truly vital forces of her people and culture."[25]
Following "the cyclic principle of African personality,"[26] she
first proceeds outward from the village and tradition and then
returns to her African heritage. Her return is thus psychologi-
cally and philosophically fulfilling. It is perhaps significant that
Ekwensi once defined African writing as "that piece of self-
expression in which the psychology behind African thought is
manifest; in which the philosophy and the pattern of culture
from which it springs can be discerned."[27] In Ekwensi's fiction
it is often by means of a circular structure that the psychology
behind African thought, and the philosophy and African pattern
of culture from which it springs, are made manifest.

All this said, Ekwensi's novels are still failures. They combine
some of the worst features of Western popular literature with
some of the least subtle techniques of African oral narrative art.
It seems that when Ekwensi is not trying to get by with cheap
effects borrowed from shoddy sources, he is laboring to make an

obvious point. Thus, rather like his heroes, he vacillates between complete Westernization and reversions to his African heritage. There would be nothing wrong with mixing foreign and native narrative traditions in a literary work, if it were artfully done. But Ekwensi lacks artistic discretion, and for a popular novelist there is no more fatal flaw.

NOTES

1 Cyprian Ekwensi, "Literary Influences on a Young Nigerian," *Times Literary Supplement*, June 4, 1964, p. 475.
2 Though not published until 1966, Cyprian Ekwensi's *Juju Rock* may have been written as many as twenty years earlier. There are references to it in *The Leopard's Claw* (London, 1950) and *The Passport of Mallam Ilia* (Cambridge, 1960), both of which were written in 1947.
3 Cyprian Ekwensi, *Juju Rock* (Lagos, 1966), p. 7.
4 *Ibid.*, p. 71.
5 Cyprian Ekwensi, *The Passport of Mallam Ilia* (Cambridge, 1960), pp. 43–44.
6 Though not published until 1962, Ekwensi's *Burning Grass* had been completed before 1950. See the unpublished dissertation (Northwestern University, 1965) by Nancy J. Schmidt, "An Anthropological Analysis of Nigerian Fiction," p. 73.
7 Cyprian Ekwensi, *Burning Grass* (London, 1962), pp. 59–60.
8 Three substantial survey articles have been written on this literature: Ulli Beier, "Public Opinion on Lovers. Popular Nigerian Literature Sold in Onitsha Market," *Black Orpheus*, No. 14 (February 1964), pp. 4–16; Donatus I. Nwoga, "Onitsha Market Literature," *Transition*, No. 19 (1965), pp. 26–33; Nancy J. Schmidt, "Nigeria: Fiction for the Average Man," *Africa Report*, 10, No. 8 (August 1965), 39–41. The fullest study of this literature to date is Emmanuel Obiechina's *Literature for the Masses: An Analytical Study of Popular Pamphleteering in Nigeria* (Enugu, 1971).
9 Cyprian Ekwensi, *When Love Whispers* (Onitsha, n.d.), p. 5.
10 *Ibid.*, p. 33.
11 In an interview published in *Afrique*, No. 24 (May 1963), p. 49, Ekwensi said, ". . . for some people [*When Love Whispers*] has become a kind of classic. Today it is still in circulation, and people

still read it before going to bed." I am grateful to Mrs. Sandy Barkan for this translation.

12 Cyprian Ekwensi, *Jagua Nana* (London, 1961), p. 126.

13 Cyprian Ekwensi, *Iska* (London, 1966), pp. 123–24.

14 Cyprian Ekwensi, *People of the City* (London, 1954), p. 50.

15 Cyprian Ekwensi, *Yaba Roundabout Murder* (Lagos, 1962), p. 17.

16 Cyprian Ekwensi, *Ikolo the Wrestler and Other Ibo Tales* (London, 1947) was later reissued under the title *The Great Elephant Bird* (London, 1965). Ekwensi also published *The Boa Suiter* (London, 1966), another collection of Ibo tales.

17 Cyprian Ekwensi, "Outlook for African Writers," *West African Review*, January 1950, p. 19.

18 Cyprian Ekwensi, *Beautiful Feathers* (London, 1963), p. 1.

19 *Ibid.*, p. 20.

20 *Ibid.*, p. 48.

21 *Ibid.*, pp. 48–49.

22 *Ibid.*, p. 160.

23 Joseph Campbell, *The Hero With a Thousand Faces* (New York, 1949). Someone more familiar with popular sex-romances than I am has informed me that this literature often exhibits what can be seen as a cyclic structure and almost always has an unmistakable moral thrust, so this pattern in Ekwensi's writing may be more popular than folkloric in origin.

24 This terminology is employed by Vladimir Propp, *Morphology of the Folktale* (Bloomington, 1958).

25 Austin J. Shelton, " 'Rebushing' or Ontological Recession to Africanism: Jagua's Return to the Village," *Présence Africaine*, No. 46 (1963), pp. 49–50.

26 Austin J. Shelton, "The Cyclic Principle of African Personality," *Présence Africaine*, No. 45 (1963), pp. 145–50.

27 Cyprian Ekwensi, "The Dilemma of the African Writer," *West African Review*, July 1956, p. 703.

28 For an attack on this essay and a more generous view of Ekwensi's literary abilities, see Ernest Emenyonu, "African literature: What does it take to be its critic?," *African Literature Today*, No. 5 (1971), pp. 1–11.

HEROES AND HERO-WORSHIP IN
NIGERIAN CHAPBOOKS

*Africa will write its own history and in both north
and south it will be a history of glory and dignity.*
PATRICE LUMUMBA

In the last twenty years Nigerian writers have produced an impressive literature in English. Much of it has been written by university graduates fluent in English and well-schooled in European literary traditions. Lacking readers and publishing houses at home, most of these writers have sought publication abroad and have addressed their works to a European audience. In Nigeria this has been a literature for the educated elite.

Alongside this highbrow literature, there has grown up a low-brow literature written, printed and published in large market towns in southern Nigeria and intended for a Nigerian reading public. Most of this indigenous market literature[1] has appeared in the form of chapbooks—inexpensive paperbound pamphlets twelve to eighty pages long, ranging in price from sixpence to three shillings. Since the late nineteen-forties, when the first Nigerian chapbooks were issued, the center of the chapbook publishing industry has been Onitsha, Nigeria's largest market town, which for many years has had a sizable literate population and an abundance of printing presses. It has been said that one can pick up one hundred to two hundred and fifty different chapbook titles in the bookstalls at Onitsha market in a single day.[2] A few of these chapbooks have been written by Nigerian university graduates and authors with international reputations (e.g., Chinua Achebe, Cyprian Ekwensi), but the majority have been produced by writers who have had no formal education beyond secondary school or, in some cases, elementary school. The chapbooks are bought and read by Nigerian townsmen—

[130]

clerks, students, traders, craftsmen, taxi drivers—who are literate in English and have developed or wish to develop a reading habit. Unlike the highbrow literature, chapbooks have always been a literature of the people, by the people, and for the people.

The contents of the chapbooks reflect the interests and concerns of Nigerian townspeople. Much of the emphasis is on education. One finds educational fact books and "how to's" such as:

> *Light to Success. General Knowledge Questions and Answers for Elementary Schools and Colleges Based on New Syllabus*
> *A Dictionary of Current Affairs and Many Things Worth Knowing*
> *How to Write Love Letters, Toasts and Business Letters*
> *How to Succeed in Life*
> *How to Know Hausa, Ibo, Yoruba and English Languages*
> *How to Write Good English and Compositions*
> *100 Riddles and Wise Sayings for Party Occasions and Enjoyments*
> *One Hundred Popular Facts About "Sex and Facts"*

One also finds moral and didactic treatises with titles like commandments or warnings:

> *Man Know Thyself*
> *Never Trust All that Love You*
> *Beware of Harlots and Many Friends. The World is Hard*
> *Man Has No Rest in His Life*
> *Money Hard to Get but Easy to Spend*
> *Drunkards Believe Bar as Heaven*
> *Life Turns Man Up and Down. Money and Girls Turn Man Up and Down*
> *Why Harlots Hate Married Men and Love Bachelors*

In addition to books of instruction and advice, there are political pamphlets (*Nigerian Political Theatre, 1923–1953*),[3] short histories (*Current History of Nigeria*), biographies of famous men (*Great Men of Ibo Land*), and books of folktales, myths, proverbs, laws and customs. A Nigerian scholar has estimated that "more than three quarters of the extant titles aim at the education of the readers."[4]

But there are also quite a few chapbooks given to fiction rather than fact, to entertainment first and enlightenment second. One finds plays, short stories, poems and novelettes not unlike some of the American "dime novels" and English "shilling shockers" and "penny dreadfuls" of a century ago. Most of them tell of love troubles in the big city. Their titles and subtitles are a fair indication of their contents:

Agnes the Faithful Lover
Disaster in the Realms of Love
Love at First, Hate at Last
Romance in a Nutshell
The True Confessions of "Folake"
Jonny the Most Worried Husband
Saturday Night Disappointment
Miss Rosy in the Romance of True Love
My Wives are in Love With My Servants
My Seven Daughters Are After Young Boys
Mabel the Sweet Honey that Poured Away
How a Passenger Collector Posed and Got a Lady Teacher in Love
Why Some Rich Men Have No Trust in Some Girls
Our Modern Ladies Characters Towards Boys (The most exciting Novel with Love letters, drama, telegrams, and campaigns of Miss Beauty to the teacher asking him to marry her)
About Husband and Wife Who Hate Themselves (It was a forced marriage made by Chief Monger, as a result of this everyday so so quarrel, so so talk, so so fight, no peace)

These gems of literature sparkle with humor and drip with sentiment. Whether they conclude happily or unhappily, there is usually a moral appended at the end for the reader's edification. From these chapbooks a great deal can be learned about contemporary social problems and human values in urban Nigeria.[5]

One type of Nigerian chapbook which merits the attention of students of African history and politics is the chapbook detailing the life and times of a leading political figure.[6] There are more than twenty of these biographical chapbooks from Onitsha alone,[7] many in the form of plays, and although few bear a date of publication, it is apparent that most of them were written in response to major political events such as elections, trials, coups and assassinations. Such chapbooks are worth studying as historical documents, for they reflect common Nigerian attitudes toward prominent political leaders.

It is not surprising that one of the favorite subjects of the Onitsha biographers is Dr. Nnamdi Azikiwe, an Onitsha Ibo who became the first President of Nigeria. Many chapbook biographies of "Zik" appeared during the fifties and at least two—*Dr. Zik in the Battle for Freedom* and *Boy's Life of Zik, the President of Nigeria Republic*—were written after independence to honor his leadership. The pamphleteers were not quite so effusive over Chief Obafemi Awolowo, a prominent Yoruba leader. Awolowo was given some attention in *Zik and Awolowo in Political Storm*, a chapbook published in Lagos in 1953 just after the Eastern Nigeria and Lagos constitutional crises, and ten years later his treason trial was dramatized in two Onitsha chapbooks, *The Famous Treason Trial of Awolowo, Enahoro and 23 Others* and *The Sorrows, Complete Treason and Last Appeal of Chief Awolowo and Others*. But although he was treated with respect in these works, it is clear that the Ibo authors did not consider him the equal of their favorite son, Azikiwe. Awolowo was simply a hot news item in 1953 and 1963 and thus mere grist for their mill.

When Nigerian pamphleteers write about famous foreign politicians, their accounts tend to be long on fancy and short on facts. For example, in Thomas Iguh's play, *The Struggles and Trial of Jomo Kenyatta*, which was published shortly after Kenyatta's release from detention in 1961, Kenyatta is pictured as a freedom fighter leading large regiments of Mau Mau troops in guerrilla warfare against white settlers and in major military campaigns against government forces. On the day Kenyatta is captured at a political rally, four thousand Kikuyu men, women and children are shot dead by government soldiers. Of course, most chapbook dramatists do not pretend to be historians. Iguh prefaces another play, *Dr. Nkrumah in the Struggle for Freedom*, with the statement that "the content of this Drama is not the exact account of the Nkrumah's Episode but a vague idea of it just as I imagine it."[8] Nearly all the chapbook plays about political figures contain similar prefaces. R. I. M. Obioha, dramatizing the assassination of Sylvanus Olympio, President of the Republic of Togo, announces in an "Author's Note" that "this drama (SYLVANUS OLYMPIO) fictitiously composed, is designed to bring home to the Reader the faint idea of the whole incident, while most of the characters in the play are imaginary beings and therefore, play no substitute to any fact in the whole episode."[9]

The few chapbooks about non-African political leaders contain some of the most fanciful interpretations of recent history. Okenwa Olisah's twelve page play, *The Statements of Hitler Before the World War*, is a hilarious farce with dialogue that is three-quarters rant. Hitler enters "in a terrible army uniform" and harangues first a crowd of Germans, then God, then his soldiers, and finally himself. Much of what he says is utter nonsense, but there are moments in his tirades on England when he is made to speak what many Nigerians would no doubt regard as truth. For example:

> "There is grave unemployment and hunger in England. She relies upon her colonial countries and that is why she hesitates too much in granting independence to them.
> England cannot do without her colonies, and she persecutes and jails freedom fighters in those her colonies. Britain indirectly practices racial discrimination. She calls Africans black monkeys. She regards blackman inferior."[10]

These words make Hitler sound like an African nationalist.

In chapbook biographies of John F. Kennedy one finds a less startling but equally interesting emphasis on Kennedy's sympathy for the American Negro and the African. In the first paragraph of *How John Kennedy Suffered in Life and Died Suddenly*, B. A. Chinaka introduces him as "the man who believed in the equality of every man irrespective of colour."[11] Pages are devoted to praising the wisdom and justice of the stands Kennedy took on issues affecting Africa. His battle for civil rights legislation is described in detail. Chinaka labors to compare Kennedy to Abraham Lincoln and concludes that "the civil rights issue, that is, his fight against racial segregation earned Kennedy the assassin's bullet."[12] Wilfred Onwuka's *The Life Story and Death of*

John Kennedy is written in a similar vein. A "Foreward" by Martin I. Ikoroji Esq. states: "If the Negro race and Africa ever had a friend, if racialists in America and Europe ever had an enemy, that friend or enemy was John Kennedy the late President of the United States of America."[13] Onwuka tells of Kennedy's early life, his education at "Princeton University," his role in the war, and his entry into politics. When Kennedy is elected President, the story suddenly shifts:

> For a long period now, the Negroes in America had been under the torture of Southern white men. . . . After a series of Ugly events, resulting from this racial and colour descrimination, the late President John Kennedy decided to do something about it in order to make the conditions of American Negroes better than before. For this, he introduced a "civil right bill" to the congress calling on the House of Representatives to make it an offence for anybody to discriminate the Negroes or torture them in any way. That civil right Bill was later passed. But the irresponsible, incompetent, and greedy white Americans were not at all that happy with President Kennedy's move to stop "Colour discrimination in America."
>
> There were, in fact too much conspiracy against him because he was stopping racial discrimination, just as there were conspiracy against Abraham Lincoln when he stopped slave trade and slavery in America.[14]

Onwuka goes on to tell how Kennedy was shot and then quotes "what President Kennedy said before his Soul left the world," a four-page deathbed oration on world brotherhood and unity terminating with the following beatitudes:

> "Blessed be the land of America"
> "Blessed be the people and rulers of the world"
> "Blessed be the soul of Abraham Lincoln who died because of slavery and slave trade abolition in 1864"
> "Blessed be my dear father and mother"
> "Blessed be my brothers and sisters"
> "Blessed be my wife and children"
> "Blessed be the American Negroes whom I am sacrificing my blood for their own safety"
> "Blessed be my soul and good bye to my friends"[15]

Onwuka describes the aftermath of the assassination and concludes by asking:

> Why did Americans not remove him from Office if they assume that he was not a good ruler instead of killing him. His effort to bring about world peace and make everyone equal to law is damaged.
> WONDERFUL! WONDERFUL! WONDERFUL!!![16]

It is clear that we cannot trust a Nigerian chapbook biography to be an accurate, objective account of a man and his times. The biographers are too inclined to ignore important facts, embroider truths, invent falsehoods, and let their imaginations run riot. This is especially true of the playwrights, who take full advantage of their right to be unfaithful to fact, but it is also true of the more serious writers who claim to have done "every thing possible to ensure accurate information."[17]

Of what use, then, are these materials as historical documents? One answer has already been suggested: they reflect common Nigerian attitudes toward prominent political leaders. But how widespread are the attitudes they reflect? Can such attitudes really be considered Nigerian attitudes or are they only Ibo attitudes or merely Onitsha Ibo attitudes? Do the writers always hold the same opinion of a particular political leader or do their opinions differ? I think it is probably true that greater differences of attitude and opinion will be found in the chapbooks about Nigerian political figures than in the chapbooks about foreign political figures. I think people in democratic nations tend to be more sharply divided in their opinions about their own national leaders than they are in their opinions about leaders of other nations. I would not expect an Ibo, a Yoruba and a Hausa, for example, to be equally enthusiastic about the leadership of, say, Chief Awolowo. But I think it is possible, even probable, that they would all have similar feelings about John F. Kennedy or Jomo Kenyatta. In every group of chapbooks that I have read about a non-Nigerian political leader, there has been a uniform opinion expressed about the leader. The "facts" about the man may vary from chapbook to chapbook but the image of the man remains the same. I think we can accept such an image as an accurate reflection of *Nigerian* attitudes toward the man even though virtually all the chapbooks projecting the image have been written by members of one tribe and have been produced in one city. The chapbooks, in other words, do mirror Nigerian public opinion about non-Nigerian leaders.

To demonstrate this I propose to examine Nigerian attitudes toward a Congolese nationalist, Patrice Lumumba, who has been the subject of more Nigerian chapbooks than any other non-Nigerian political leader. At least ten chapbooks about Lumumba appeared in the years following his sudden death in 1961.[18] I have been able to examine seven of these as well as one about Moise Tshombe[19] which was produced as a sequel to a chapbook on Lumumba. Since six of these eight are written in dramatic form, a few preliminary remarks will be made on chapbooks as plays.

First, it must be admitted that chapbook plays are not very skillfully written. Most of the authors have learned the basic mechanics of playwriting; they divide their plays into acts and scenes and often include elaborate stage directions and descriptions of setting. Their characters occasionally speak in monologues and asides, and when a character leaves the stage, his departure is commonly celebrated with the word "EXEUNT," whether he leaves alone or with others. But although these would-be playwrights have obviously learned much about how to write a play, they have learned very little about how to make a play. They appear to know nothing at all about presenting information through action, about varying mood and tempo, about building to a climax. Their only intention seems to be to fill up every scene with something highly dramatic, something memorable. As a result, the plays are full of sound and fury— heated arguments, bombastic speeches, battles, riots, acrobatics —but they are devoid of those subtler rhythms and overtones that can make a play a work of art.

Of course, one shouldn't expect these plays to be works of art. They are meant merely as diversions. In one author's preface we read: "This drama . . . is an imaginary story compiled to interest the reader for his leisure and amusement. . . . It is my humble belief that this Drama with all its mistakes will still amuse and entertain the reader."[20]

The prefaces also reveal that the playwrights want their plays to be performed and are willing to forego royalties:

Schools, Clubs and Societies are free to stage the play if so desired.[21]

The play is written in simple language to make it possible for school children to perform it.[22]

. . . groups, clubs and all are permitted to use it in any type of play, such as concert, etc., if they really have interest in it.[23]

But it is difficult to imagine how some of the happenings in these plays could be presented on stage. Thomas Iguh's *The Last Days of Lumumba* (*The Late Lion of the Congo*), for example, contains the following stage directions:

At this stage a group of about two thousand Lumumbists gather outside Patrice Lumumba's house carrying banners, palm leaves and a coffin.

At this stage Patrice Lumumba mounts on the back of his horse dressed in the uniform of a Commander in Chief armed with a sword and a spear. He is led in a very long procession to the market square.

At this stage, the angry crowd surged to the road and halt the car. They draw out the occupants and slash them to pieces. They march home with war songs while parts of the bodies of the butchered Belgians are conspicuously displayed in front of the informal procession.

Over a million Lumumbists gather around the court.

(They are all stripped naked and punished severely)[24]

Needless to say, such a play would tax the ingenuity of the most resourceful director.[25]

The most obvious literary influence on Onitsha chapbook plays has been Shakespeare. The Lumumba plays ring with echoes from *Julius Caesar*, *Macbeth* and *The Merchant of Venice*.

"Comrades Mpolo, Okito and the rest, lend me your ears. . . ."[26]
"Peace loh! Lumumba speaks!"[27]
"The evil that men do lives after them!"[28]
"A coward dies seven times before his death."[29]

[138]

"Kasavubu, be a green snake in the green grass."[30]
"But come what may, the night is long that never finds the day!"[31]
"The Quality of Mercy is not Strained."[32]
"On what compulsion must I! Tell me!"[33]

One also finds crowd scenes in which "CITIZENS" respond in chorus or individually to Lumumba's oratory. In one play a "spirit" warns Lumumba to send his children to Egypt before troops come to arrest him.[34] In another, the ghosts of Lumumba, Okito and Mpolo come back to haunt the "conspirators"—Tshombe, Kasavubu, and Mobutu.[35] Since every Nigerian secondary schoolboy is required to study at least one Shakespearean play, often *Julius Caesar*, it can be assumed that these literary allusions are not lost on many readers.

Another source of influence on these plays has been the Bible. One finds the characters uttering such words as:

". . . verily I say. . . ."[36]
". . . revengeance shall be mine."[37]
"How are the mighty fallen."[38]
". . . into thy hand I commend my spirit."[39]

Kasavubu is called "another Judas who can betray his own Lord,"[40] and the removal of Lumumba's children to Cairo is compared to flights into Egypt recorded in the Bible.[41] In whatever struggles ensue, God invariably fights on Lumumba's side.

There are a number of allusions and quotations in these plays which reflect the wide if somewhat eclectic reading of the authors. Thomas Iguh's *The Last Days of Lumumba*, for example, contains quotations from Winston Churchill, Patrick Henry, Booker T. Washington, "Mahatmer Ghandi," and an unidentified "English Author." In Ogali A. Ogali's *Patrice Lumumba*, the authors quoted are respectable nineteenth-century literary figures—Oliver Wendell Holmes, Sir Walter Scott, William Ernest Henley and James Russell Lowell. Nearly all of these Anglo-American quotations are put in the mouth of Patrice Lumumba, a French-speaking Congolese.

A generous sprinkling of English proverbs, idioms, and

clichés can be found in every play. Some of them are given interesting new twists:

> ". . . let us call a spade a spade and not a fork."[42]
> ". . . it is not wise for one to hook in troubled water."[43]
> ". . . one can't eat his cake and have it back again."[44]
> ". . . pay the shameless traitors back in their own coins."[45]
> "Come on comrades! Let's be on the war path."[46]

Occasionally one comes across an amusing misprint such as "the joke of imperialism"[47] or "Katanga . . . the bad rock of Congo wealth."[48] But the most delightful surprises are the new turns of phrase which these writers wrench out of the English language.

> "What ever you do to me now will never move me from my stand. It will rather serve as a lubricant to my elbows."[49]
> ". . . it bothers my brain heavily. . . ."[50]
> "It beats my imagination very much. . . ."[51]

At its best this kind of writing is fresh, vigorous and imaginative. At its worst it is merely incomprehensible. But good or bad, deliberate or accidental, borrowed or invented, features of chapbook style should be studied as carefully as features of chapbook form or content. I suspect that writers who approach a foreign language with so much zest and audacity, who do not bother to learn all the niceties of grammar, spelling and punctuation, who simply rip into English and let the splinters fly, will be equally bold and original, equally reckless, and equally given to error and overstatement in the views they express about foreign political heroes. Certainly this seems to be the case with the writers who have written chapbooks about Patrice Lumumba.

Of all the images of Lumumba in the chapbooks, the most persistent is the image of Lumumba as Caesar. We have already noted lines parroted from Shakespeare's *Julius Caesar*, the main source of inspiration for this image. Scenes are borrowed too, and several playwrights go so far as to cast Mrs. Lumumba in the role of Calpurnia. Felix N. Stephen's *The Trials and Death of Lumumba* contains a scene in which Mrs. Lumumba and her husband converse before he goes off to parliament. She expresses concern about his safety and he answers by boasting of his invincibility. The scene is closely modeled on one in Shakespeare's plays, and to ensure that everyone will see the parallel, the playwright has Mrs. Lumumba say in a closing soliloquy:

> "O! Eh! I now remember Julius Caesar, a great Man, was assassinated by his own people. Before then, there was a type of exchange of opinion between him and his wife. He defied all suggestion and then, proceeded to where he finally met his doom." [52]

After Lumumba's arrest Mrs. Lumumba remembers their conversation this way:

> "When my husband was going away to the parliament, I warned him to be careful of Kasavubu and Tshombe. For these men are dangerous and do not seem to be working for his own good. I even went up to the extent of recalling his memory to the death of Caesar, which stemmed mainly from the plot by his assumed friends." [53]

Other playwrights also single out Tshombe and Kasavubu as the villains who "like Brutus and Cassius of Old, conspired against Lumumba and assassinated him. . . ." [54] Mobutu is identified as another conspirator, albeit sometimes a remorseful one. [55]

In two chapbook plays we find an image of Lumumba as Christ. In Ogali A. Ogali's *Patrice Lumumba*, Lumumba admonishes his captors with the following words:

> "You have all sold our hard won freedom back to Belgium and Western Powers. I know you have all vowed to treat me shamefully as did the Jews to our Saviour. . . . You have sold the Republic of Congo to Belgium and the Western Powers for thirty pieces of silver. But was the Son of Man not sold for that amount by his people?" [56]

And when Tshombe later slaps him, Lumumba asks, "Was Jesus not slapped even by those who dared not tread where he did?" [57] Another playwright has Lumumba say, "Tshombe and Kasavubu, you now torture me after I had won freedom for you. I do not regret it because in a like manner, mankind treated our

Saviour Jesus Christ."[58] In most of the plays Lumumba is made to suffer many indignities and much physical torture before he is put to death.

· Between Caesar the superman and Christ the divinity there lies a middle ground occupied by saints and martyrs. Lumumba is placed there by several playwrights, who speak of him as "The Political Martyr of Congo"[59] and "a proclaimed saint of African emancipation."[60] Every chapbook about Lumumba adds lustre to this image by stressing his numerous ordeals, his stoical acceptance of death, and his assurance of immortality. One chapbook is entitled *The Trials of Lumumba, Jomo Kenyatta and St. Paul*.[61]

Slightly less ethereal and far more mundane is the image of Lumumba as a great nationalist. There is a tendency to identify him with great leaders who strove for national independence or national unity. In the plays it is Lumumba himself who makes these equations:

"I have fought successfully for the independence of my country. Was Ghandi not killed after securing the independence of India? I am now fighting for the Union and was Abraham Lincoln not killed after maintaining America's Union?"[62]

In another play Lumumba says:

"The worst you can do is to kill me and that won't bother me at all. Was Mahatma Ghandi of India not killed by the people he spent his life saving for? Was Solomon Bendaraniake of Ceylon not shot to death by the people for whom he secured Freedom?"[63]

Even Lumumba's enemies recognize his outstanding qualities of leadership. In one play Kasavubu declares that "Patrice Lumumba is very dynamic and it is through him that the personality of this country can be projected to the outside world."[64] In every play it is Lumumba's "dynamism" that makes him an outstanding nationalist leader.

Contained in every one of these images is the suggestion that Patrice Lumumba is one of the immortals. It is believed that his words, his deeds, his spirit, his "personality" will not perish with him but will live forever in the hearts and minds of men and in the history books of the Congo. Lumumba himself is pictured as believing this:

"My name must go down in history, as a hero. Generations upon generations, will read of me and thus, have an inspiration."[65]

"I have won the Independence for my country and should I die now, Congo's history must never be complete without Lumumba's name being prominently and colourfully written."[66]

"Though my head is going to be cut off, my name will remain green in the panteon of Congo history! . . . I repeat; though my head is going to be cut off, my name will be written in diamond letters when the History of the Congo will come to be written."[67]

How the history of the Congo will be written one hundred years from now remains to be seen, but it appears likely that then as now the average Nigerian citizen will insist that "the Congolese history would never be interesting, correct and readable, without Lumumba's name well decorated. . . ."[68] Apotheosis, after all, is an irreversible phenomenon. A man popularly regarded as a Caesar, a Christ, a saint and martyr, a great nationalist, and an immortal will not shrink in stature with the passage of time.

How future generations will regard Lumumba's enemies is a different question. One or two who are not yet safely dead still have a chance to redeem themselves. This makes it more difficult to spin durable legends about them. In all the chapbooks Tshombe, Kasavubu and Mobutu are pictured as conspirators, traitors, and stooges or puppets of the imperialists, but in at least one, Felix N. Stephen's *How Tshombe and Mobutu Regretted After the Death of Mr. Lumumba*, they are made to appear sorry for their misdeeds.

A more detestable enemy, according to some of the chapbooks, is the United Nations. One playwright prefaces his play with the words:

Read on and spend an hour with me in the riot torn Republic of Congo where murderers and traitors can go free in the very nose of the supreme council of the world, the infamous UNITED NATIONS ORGANIZATION![69]

In the same play, Mrs. Lumumba, hearing of her husband's death, shouts, "The United Nations has killed him."[70] In one of the chapbook biographies Lumumba's greatest grievance against the U.N. is spelled out in a letter Lumumba is said to have written to his wife:

. . . never trust the protection of the United Nations. When the Congo crisis started, I invited the United Nations to come and intervene. The U.N. arrived and teamed up against me. As you know, they are indirectly supporting President Kasavubu.[71]

In other words, the U.N. betrayed Lumumba. It proved to be another false friend. One playwright tries to bring the message closer to home by having Lumumba's brother Albert reproach Dag Hammarskjöld with these words:

"Were you not invited here to maintain the peace and security of Congo? Was it not Lumumba who invited you? When Mobutu and his gang got hold of some white men, did you not send the Nigerian troops of the United Nations to set them free and when Lumumba and his two ministers were taken prisoners, did you not say it was Congo's internal affairs oh you die hard imperialist, accompliced murderer of the first grade!"[72]

Thus Lumumba is portrayed as a hero who fought against over-whelming odds, against both a coalition of Congolese powers and a coalition of world powers. He was a great man, he fought for a good cause, he was betrayed, he suffered and he died. This is the chapbook legend of Lumumba.

But how widespread is this legend in Nigeria? How popular are these images of Lumumba and his enemies? To answer such questions we need only to examine a sample of the opinions expressed about Lumumba and the Congo situation in various Nigerian newspapers in the months following the announce-ment of Lumumba's death. It should be remembered that most of the Lumumba chapbooks were being written at this time.

The newspapers reveal that Nigerians reacted strongly to the murder of Lumumba. Funeral marches and protest demonstrations were held in cities all over the country. Whites were attacked and their cars damaged in a riot that broke out in front of the United States Embassy in Lagos. Politicians demanded that Nigeria break off diplomatic relations with Belgium and withdraw Nigerian troops from the U.N. peace-keeping force in the Congo. Women's groups organized committees to collect clothes for Lumumba's wife and children.

The newspapers became cluttered with articles, editorials, letters, eulogies and sonnets honoring Lumumba. Most of these tributes were swollen with emotion and windy with rhetoric. R. S. O. Erumagborie, a Yoruba writing in Lagos' *West African Pilot*, predicted that the murderers of Lumumba would not go unpunished: ". . . like Caesar, the ghost of Patrice Lumumba shall hunt these devil-incarnates from Stanleyville to Leopoldville, from Manono to Elizabethville from Washington to Brussels and from London to Paris, seeking revenge."[73] Andy Uchenna Anarodo, an Ibo writing in Zaria's *Nigerian Citizen*, echoed a few of Mark Antony's most famous lines: "If Lumumba has been ambitious, then it is to be argued, but if he has been fighting a genuine cause history shall prove him right, so let it be with Lumumba."[74]

While some Nigerians gave unto Lumumba what was Caesar's, others gave unto Lumumba what was Christ's. Chief Fred U. Anyiam, an Ibo politician from Orlu, declared in the *West African Pilot* that the murder of Lumumba was a monstrous crime: "This barbarous act is only second to the brutality and crucifixion of our Lord Jesus. . . ."[70] A year later, S. O. Erengwa, an Ibo from Enugu, made a similar comparison when he commemorated the first anniversary of Lumumba's death in a letter to the same newspaper:

Like the Christ of old, you came to your people but your people knew you not. You redeemed them from slavery, but they turned round to betray you. On a platter of gold did you bring Independence to them, but they turned to make you a victim of the

Independence. You sought unity for your Congo, but they chose to sacrifice you on the alter of chaos.[76]

Headlines and editorials in Nigerian newspapers pronounced Lumumba a martyr and a saint. A Yoruba poet wrote:

Brave Hero Patrice Lumumba! Rest in Peace.
With Martyrs of all Nations and all Ages, Rest![77]

One of the demonstrators in a Kano rally carried a sign with the inscription, "St. Lumumba a Martyr."[78] A Hausa in Zaria, remembering Ireland's devotion to St. Patrick suggested: "Now we have another St. Patrick, for it is as a saint that Patrice Lumumba must appear to many of his countrymen. Perhaps the Congo and Ireland will, one day, unite in the adoption of the Saint's feast as a national holiday."[79]

Lumumba was also applauded as a great nationalist. In a letter to the *West African Pilot* a Midwesterner lamented that "Africa has lost a Lincoln."[80] A few days later a letter from a Yaba Ibo asked, "What sins did Lumumba commit? None, other than ideals of Abraham Lincoln who is now being canonized."[81] A Yoruba writing in Zaria's *Nigerian Citizen* claimed that "to all Africans, Mr. Lumumba symbolizes African nationalism."[82] An Ibo writer identified Lumumba as "one of the greatest African nationalists that the present generation and posterity will read of in the history of Africa."[83]

Lumumba was already thought to be immortal. The day after his death was announced the Kano *Daily Comet* reported that he "is still living in the hearts of African people and the freedom loving world."[84] An Ibo poet contributed a poem to the *West African Pilot* entitled "The Spirit of Patrice Lumumba Lives."[85] In the Lagos *Daily Express* an Ibo writer declared that "Lumumba is a name that lives as long as there is Africa. Lumumba's soul keeps marching on."[86]

Lumumba's enemies were denounced in every newspaper. In Ibadan's *Nigerian Tribune* a Yoruba regretted that "the blood of these three sons of Africa [Lumumba, Okito, Mpolo] has been used to water the tree of imperialism and fellow Africans have been used to obtain this objective. Oh, these greedy Africans who sold their birth right for a mess of porridge!"[87] One of the letters to the editor of Kano's *Daily Comet* prophesied that "like Brutus and Casius Tshombe, Kasavubu and Mobutu will run from pillar to post until they find themselves a rendezvous with death."[88]

However, the most sinister of Lumumba's enemies was not a Congolese leader. An editorial in the *West African Pilot* put forward the view that "Lumumba was hacked to death by his political adversaries on the instigation of the imperialists with the connivance of the United Nations."[89] A Hausa writing in Zaria's *Nigerian Citizen* felt that "the murder of Mr. Lumumba under the Blue Flag of the United Nations is the greatest crime in nature."[90] An Ibo writer deplored the U.N.'s duplicity: "The United Nations . . . turned out to be the instrument for the deposition and fall of the person who had invited them."[91] Lumumba was a man betrayed.

Nigerian newspapers thus confirm that the legend of Lumumba presented in the chapbooks was a widespread and popular legend in Nigeria months before the first Lumumba chapbooks were published. It was a legend that grew up immediately after the announcement of Lumumba's death and that captured the imagination of the average Nigerian, regardless of his tribe or political affiliation. In the East, in the West, and in the North, Lumumba was deemed a Caesar, a Christ, a saint and martyr, a great nationalist, an immortal, and a man foully betrayed. In the chapbooks he was deemed so too. The chapbooks therefore accurately reflect common Nigerian attitudes toward Lumumba.

Every nation must have its heroes, and not every hero need be a native son. A nation will adopt a foreign hero as its own if that hero symbolizes its own national ideals and aspirations. Patrice Lumumba had fought to end colonial domination and to achieve national unity in the Congo. Nigerians had fought and were fighting for the same goals in Nigeria. What made Lumumba seem a greater hero than other African nationalists, such as Nkrumah and Kenyatta, was his untimely death. He died in the struggle. This made him the noblest nationalist of them all. This made him a legend. And this made him the subject of so many Nigerian chapbooks.

NOTES

1 The fullest study of this literature is Emmanuel Obiechina's *Literature for the Masses: An Analytical Study of Popular Pamphleteering in Nigeria* (Enugu, 1971). See also: Ulli Beier, "Public Opinion on Lovers. Popular Nigerian Literature Sold in Onitsha Market," *Black Orpheus*, No. 14 (February 1964), pp. 4–16; Donatus I. Nwoga, "Onitsha Market Literature," *Transition*, No. 19 (1965), pp. 26–33; Nancy J. Schmidt, "Nigeria: Fiction for the Average Man," *Africa Report*, 10, No. 8 (August 1965), 39–41. Briefer accounts have been offered by Thomas R. Buckman, "Bookstalls in an African Market: Onitsha, Eastern Nigeria," *Books and Libraries at the University of Kansas*, 4, No. 2 (November 31, 1966), 1–2; J. O. Reed, "Africa's Market Literature," *Nation*, 196 (June 15, 1963), 509–10; Peter Young, "A Note from Onitsha," *Bulletin of the Association for African Literature in English*, No. 4 (March 1966), pp. 37–40; and "Writing in West Africa. A Chance to Adapt and to Experiment," *Times Literary Supplement*, August 10, 1962, pp. 570–01.

2 Beier, "Public Opinion on Lovers," p. 4; Nwoga, "Onitsha Market Literature," p. 26.

3 A list of such pamphlets can be found in James S. Coleman's *Nigeria: Background to Nationalism* (Berkeley and Los Angeles, 1963), pp. 489–95. Coleman has drawn on Ruth Perry, "A Preliminary Bibliography of the Literature of Nationalism in Nigeria" (mimeographed, 1955).

4 Nwoga, p. 27.

5 In an unpublished doctoral dissertation Nancy J. Schmidt has examined this literature from an anthropological point of view: "An Anthropological Analysis of Nigerian Fiction" (Northwestern University, 1965).

6 I am aware of only one detailed study of this type of chapbook: K. W. J. Post, "Nigerian Pamphleteers and the Congo," *Journal of Modern African Studies*, 2, No. 3 (November 1964), 405–13. In what follows I am very much in debt to Professor Post.

7 See the bibliography in Coleman, *Nigeria*, and the bibliography attached. The plays are also listed in my "A Preliminary Checklist of Nigerian Drama in English," *Afro-Asian Theatre Bulletin*, 2, No. 2 (February 1967), 16–21.

8 Thomas Iguh, *Dr. Nkrumah in the Struggle for Freedom* (Onitsha, n.d.), p. 4. In all quotations the spelling, grammar and punctuation have been left as in the original.

9 R. I. M. Obioha, *Sylvanus Olympio* (Onitsha, 1964), p. 3.

10 Okenwa Olisah, *The Statements of Hitler Before the World War* (Onitsha, n.d.), p. 6.

11 B. A. Chinaka, *How John Kennedy Suffered in Life and Died Suddenly* (Onitsha, n.d.), p. 4.

12 *Ibid.*, p. 34.

13 Wilfred Onwuka, *The Life Story and Death of John Kennedy* (Onitsha, n.d.), p. 4.

14 *Ibid.*, pp. 17–19.

15 *Ibid.*, p. 22.

16 *Ibid.*, p. 52.

17 Okenwa Olisah, *The Life Story and Death of Mr. Lumumba* (Onitsha, n.d.), p. 3.

18 Besides those listed in the bibliography I have seen references to Ogali A. Ogali, *The Ghost of Lumumba* (Onitsha, n.d.), advertised in Ogali A. Ogali, *Patrice Lumumba* (Onitsha, 1961), p. 2; Felix N. Stephen, *The Sorrows of Patrice Lumumba* (Onitsha, n.d.), listed in Janheinz Jahn, *A Bibliography of Neo-African Literature* (London, 1965), p. 61; and Felix N. Stephen, *The Trials of Lumumba, Jomo Kenyatta and St. Paul* (Onitsha, n.d.), cited in Post, "Nigerian Pamphleteers," p. 408.

19 Thomas O. Iguh, *Tshombe of Katanga* (Onitsha, n.d.).

20 *Ibid.*, p. 3.

21 Ogali A. Ogali, *Patrice Lumumba* (Onitsha, 1961), p. 5.

22 Michael Urinrin Lakpah, *The Blood of Lumumba* (Warri, 1961), p. 1. Lakpah plagiarizes Ogali, *supra*.

23 Iguh, *Tshombe*, p. 4.

24 Thomas Iguh, *The Last Days of Lumumba* (*The Late Lion of the Congo*) (Onitsha, n.d.), pp. 10, 11, 15, 18, 53.

25 According to reports from eyewitnesses, this play has been performed in both Nigeria and Ghana. See the notes in Post, "Nigerian Pamphleteers," pp. 405 and 411. A returned Peace Corps volunteer told me she saw the play performed by schoolboys in Ghana.

26 Iguh, *Last Days*, p. 8.

27 *Ibid.*, p. 12.

28 *Ibid.*, p. 56. Cf. Ogali, *Patrice Lumumba*, p. 40, and Okenwa Olisa, *How Lumumba Suffered in Life and Died in Katanga* (Onitsha, n.d.), p. 8.

29 Ogali, *Patrice Lumumba*, p. 25.

30 *Ibid.*, p. 13.
31 *Ibid.*, p. 14.
32 Iguh, *Last Days*, p. 32.
33 *Ibid.*, pp. 16, 54.
34 *Ibid.*, pp. 48–49.
35 Felix N. Stephen, *How Tshombe and Mobutu Regretted After the Death of Mr. Lumumba* (Onitsha, n.d.), pp. 30–33.
36 Ogali, *Patrice Lumumba*, p. 25.
37 *Ibid.*, p. 26.
38 Iguh, *Last Days*, p. 56.
39 *Ibid.*, p. 23.
40 Ogali, *Patrice Lumumba*, p. 15.
41 *Ibid.*, pp. 26–27.
42 Iguh, *Tshombe*, p. 23.
43 *Ibid.*, p. 32.
44 Iguh, *Last Days*, p. 35. Cf. Ogali, *Patrice Lumumba*, p. 10.
45 *Ibid.*, p. 51. Cf. Ogali, *Patrice Lumumba*, p. 14.
46 *Ibid.*, p. 63.
47 Olisah, *The Life Story*, p. 25.
48 Iguh, *Last Days*, p. 40.
49 *Ibid.*, p. 26.
50 Iguh, *Tshombe*, p. 31.
51 Olisah, *The Life Story*, p. 22.
52 Felix N. Stephen, *The Trials and Death of Lumumba* (Onitsha, n.d.), pp. 14–15.
53 *Ibid.*, pp. 24–25.
54 Lakpah, *Blood of Lumumba*, p. 2.
55 See especially Stephen, *How Tshombe*, pp. 34–35.
56 Ogali, *Patrice Lumumba*, p. 16.
57 *Ibid.*, p. 29.
58 Lakpah, *Blood of Lumumba*, p. 13.
59 *Ibid.*, p. 1.
60 Ogali, *Patrice Lumumba*, p. 4.
61 See footnote 18.
62 Ogali, *Patrice Lumumba*, pp. 25–26.
63 Iguh, *Last Days*, p. 54.
64 Stephen, *How Tshombe*, p. 15.
65 Stephen, *Trials and Death*, p. 14.
66 Ogali, *Patrice Lumumba*, p. 30.
67 Iguh, *Last Days*, p. 57.
68 Okenwa Olisa, *How Lumumba Suffered in Life and Died in Katanga* (Onitsha, n.d.), p. 7.
69 Ogali, *Patrice Lumumba*, p. 4.
70 *Ibid.*, p. 40.
71 Olisa, *How Lumumba Suffered*, p. 4.
72 Ogali, *Patrice Lumumba*, p. 38.
73 R. S. O. Erumagborie, *West African Pilot*, March 2, 1961, p. 4.

I am grateful to Mr. Oyekan Owomoyela and Mrs. Helen Peters, formerly of the University of California at Los Angeles, and to Professor Sunday O. Anozie of State University College, New Paltz, New York, for helping me to identify Yoruba, Ibo and Hausa names.

74 Andy Uchenna Anarodo, *Nigerian Citizen*, February 22, 1961, p. 4.
75 Fred U. Anyiam, *West African Pilot*, February 18, 1961, p. 5.
76 S. O. Erengwa, *West African Pilot*, February 19, 1962, p. 3. Also quoted in Post, "Nigerian Pamphleteers," p. 406.
77 Olatunde Lawrence, *West African Pilot*, February 17, 1961, p. 5.
78 *Daily Comet*, February 27, 1961, p. 1.
79 Adamu Safar, *Nigerian Citizen*, February 22, 1961, p. 5.
80 E. Erhisere, *West African Pilot*, February 22, 1961, p. 4.
81 Stephen C. Oguike, *West African Pilot*, February 25, 1961, p. 4.
82 Tobi Dafe O. O. Jibowu, *Nigerian Citzen*, March 4, 1961, p. 4.
83 Paully Amadi, *West African Pilot*, March 13, 1961, p. 4.
84 *Daily Comet*, February 15, 1961, p. 1.
85 Dennis Osadebay, *West African Pilot*, February 15, 1961, p. 5.
86 Mazi G. C. Opara, *Daily Express*, March 1, 1961, p. 4.
87 Ayo Adebayo, *Nigerian Tribune*, February 18, 1961, p. 4.
88 Peter Onu, *Daily Comet*, February 24, 1961, p. 4.
89 *West African Pilot*, February 16, 1961, p. 4.
90 Y. N. Abubakar, *Nigerian Citizen*, February 22, 1961, p. 4.
91 G. U. M. Nwagbara, *West African Pilot*, February 17, 1961, p. 4.

BIBLIOGRAPHY OF CHAPBOOKS CONSULTED

Aririguzo, Cyril N. *Steps for the Freedom of Nigeria*. Onitsha, n.d.
Chinaka, B. A. *How John Kennedy Suffered In Life and Died Suddenly*. Onitsha, n.d.
Iguh, Thomas Orlando. *Dr. Nkrumah in the Struggle for Freedom*. Onitsha, n.d.
— *Dr. Zik in the Battle for Freedom*. Onitsha, 1961.
— *The Last Days of Lumumba (The Late Lion of the Congo)*. Onitsha, n.d.
— *The Sorrows, Complete Treason and Last Appeal of Chief Awolowo and Others*. Onitsha, n.d.
— *The Struggles and Trial of Jomo Kenyatta*. Onitsha, n.d.
— *Tshombe of Katanga*. Onitsha, n.d.
Izuogu, Okwu. *Heroes of New Africa. Zik. Genius of To-day*. Onitsha, n.d.

Lakpah, Michael Urinrin. *The Blood of Lumumba*. Warri, 1961.

Mbadugha, Chike. *Zik of Africa. His Political Struggles for Freedom of the Black Race*. Onitsha, 1958.

Obioha, R. I. M. *Sylvanus Olympio*. Onitsha, 1964.

Ogali, Ogali A. *Patrice Lumumba*. Onitsha, 1961.

Okenwa, M. *Boy's Life of Zik, the President of Nigeria Republic*. Onitsha, n.d.

Olisah (Olisa), Okenwa. *How Lumumba Suffered in Life and Died in Katanga*. Onitsha, n.d.

— *The Life Story and Death of Mr. Lumumba*. Onitsha, n.d.

— *The Statements of Hitler Before the World War*. Onitsha, n.d.

Onokpasa, B. E. *The Hero of Sharpeville*. Ibadan, n.d.

Onwuka, Wilfred. *The Famous Treason Trial of Awolowo, Enahoro and 23 Others*. Onitsha, n.d.

— *The Life Story and Death of John Kennedy*. Onitsha, n.d.

Stephen, Felix N. *How Tshombe and Mobutu Regretted After the Death of Mr. Lumumba*. Onitsha, n.d.

— *The Trials and Death of Lumumba*. Onitsha, n.d.

Uwanaka, Charles U. *Zik and Awolowo in Political Storm*. Lagos, 1953 (reprinted Onitsha, 1960).

CHARACTERISTICS OF YORUBA AND IBO PROSE STYLES IN ENGLISH

Critics of African literature tend to be either racists, nationalists or individualists. The racists devoutly believe in the *africanité* of African literature and usually seek to demonstrate that black African writers think alike, feel alike, and therefore write alike. They do not particularly care where in sub-Saharan Africa a writer lives or what his background happens to be or which language or literary form he chooses to employ; so long as he is black and African his writing is regarded as an expression of *négritude*, a verbal manifestation of the negro African soul. To racist critics the writer's pigmentation is virtually all that matters. Nationalist critics, on the other hand, are preoccupied with mapping the geography of African literature. They like to generalize about the decline of South African short fiction, the coming-of-age of Nigerian drama, the emergence of Ghanaian writing, or the end of the literary drought in East Africa. Each nation or region is presumed capable of producing a distinctive literature of its own, a literature conveniently contained within the arbitrary territorial boundaries drawn by the former colonial powers. At least one critic has already sought to define the national character of the literature written in the southern half of Nigeria,[1] and similar efforts at legitimizing literary nationalism in other parts of Africa can be expected as soon as there is enough literature available for analysis. A formal declaration of literary independence is normally based on the assumption that writers in a given country have more in common with one another than they do with writers in other countries. Thus, unlike the racist critic who looks only for similarities, the ardent nationalist critic usually looks for both similarities and differences—similarities between individual writers from the same country and differences between groups of writers from different countries. The individualist critic, to complete the trichotomy, concerns himself primarily with differences, for he is interested in defining the unique genius of the individual writer. What is most important to this critic is not the writer's race or nationality or resemblance to other authors but the full range and magnitude of his artistic achievement as measured by the fresh insights contained in his works. It is assumed that every writer has something different to say and says it in his own special way. So while the racist searches for brotherhood under the skin and the nationalist looks for brotherhood under the flag, the individualist critic seeks to discover the originality of the isolated artist.

Many critics will object to this crude typology and protest against such unpleasant-sounding names. The individualists would no doubt prefer to be described as New Critics, the nationalists probably fancy themselves literary historians, and the racists may parade as pan-African humanists. Let those who are dissatisfied with these names invent others more to their liking. The fact remains that a great deal of the criticism written on African literature has been based on assumptions about the author's race, nationality or individuality. Of course, there is nothing wrong with making such assumptions. Often they must be made in order for the critic to make some sense of the works with which he is dealing. But African literature has grown so huge in recent years that it now invites new critical approaches based on new sets of assumptions. The critic who finds a new means of entry into the literature may make better progress toward a deepened understanding of what he reads than did many of his predecessors.

One type of critic needed today is the tribalist (those who object to this term may substitute "ethnoaesthetician" or another euphemism). Such a critic would examine African literature from an ethnic point of view, noting significant similarities and differences in the content, structure and style of works by writers from various African tribes. His aim would be to define the ethnicity[2] of each tribe's literature in order to test the validity of the assumption that every tribe or group of related tribes produces a distinctive literature, even when its writers express themselves in a foreign language. In a sense the tribalist critic could be considered a cross between the racist and the nationalist but one who deals with smaller, more coherent ethnic units. Confronted with a work like *The Palm-Wine Drinkard*, for example, he would not be drawn off into discussions of its Africanness or Nigerianness but would concentrate on trying to ascertain its quintessential Yorubaness by comparing it with other works by Yoruba writers. To strengthen his case he might also contrast it with African literary works written by non-Yorubas.

Anthropological training would be a great asset to the tribalist critic[3] but not an absolute necessity. Using the techniques of comparative literature he could make perfectly valid distinctions between two or more literatures without reference to the cultures from which these literatures sprung. For example, on the level of style he might attempt to discriminate between the ways in which Ijaw and Zulu writers express themselves in English. If he happened to be fluent in both Ijaw and Zulu and familiar with storytelling traditions in these tribes, he could draw upon linguistic and cultural evidence to support his argument. But if he knew nothing of the language and culture of either tribe and could still clearly distinguish between the styles of Ijaw and Zulu writers, his argument would be no less persuasive.

To demonstrate how a tribalist critic might proceed to make a stylistic comparison without recourse to anthropological evidence, I propose to examine characteristic features of Yoruba and Ibo prose styles in English. My basic assumption is that a person's first language usually influences the manner in which he expresses himself in a second. From this it follows that two people with different first languages will speak the same second language differently. To put it more concretely, a native speaker of Yoruba and a native speaker of Ibo will not express

[155]

themselves in English in quite the same way. But two native speakers of Yoruba might. And the native speaker of English would have no difficulty sorting out the Ibos from the Yorubas if he were sufficiently attuned to their characteristic stylistic differences. It therefore seems quite legitimate for literary critics to search for tribal prose styles in African literature in English without consulting the anthropologists.

Let us begin with Chief Daniel Olorunfemi Fagunwa, the Yoruba writer who before his death in 1963 produced five novels, a collection of stories, two travel books, and a series of graded readers for use in schools. Fagunwa wrote in Yoruba, but recent translations of his fiction[4] place later Yoruba writing in English in an interesting perspective. Here is a typical passage from the opening pages of Fagunwa's first novel, *Ogboju Ode Ninu Igbo Irunmale* (1938), which Wole Soyinka has translated under the title *The Forest of a Thousand Daemons* (1968):

> My name is Akara-ogun, Compound-of-Spells, one of the formidable hunters of a bygone age. My own father was a hunter, he was also a great one for medicines and spells. He had a thousand powder gourdlets, eight hundred *ato*, and his amulets numbered six hundred. Two hundred and sixty incubi lived in that house and the birds of divination were without number. It was the spirits who guarded the house when he was away, and no one dared enter that house when my father was absent—it was unthinkable. But deep as he was in the art of the supernatural, he was no match for my mother, for she was a deep seasoned witch from the cauldrons of hell.[5]

Notice the string of hyperboles, the concern with number and amount, the climactic contrast. Ulli Beier has pointed out that "Fagunwa is fond of rhetoric. He likes words. He likes to pile them up, say the same thing over and over again in infinite variation. He is a master of rhetoric, who can make repetitions and variations swing in a mounting rhythm, like Yoruba drumming."[6] Here is another example, this one taken from Fagunwa's second novel, *Igbo Olodumare* (1948), in which the same narrator appears:

I am truly Akara-Ogun, the father who begot me was an herbalist and he was a *father of secrets* also; and we were up to our necks in medicine in our house and in fact there were strange objects in the dark corners of the rooms, and powerful medicines were kept in the ceiling, and various living creatures were caged in our backyard.

And those who were epileptics were cured by my father, those who had guinea worms were healed by him also, and thousands of lepers were transformed into well beloved people in our house. And my father punished small pox, and he assaulted under-nourishment; he spoiled the reputation of rheumatism and turned stomach trouble into a pauper. And headache became like a powerless child and back-ache became speechless, and cough had to go into hiding and chest pains took to their legs, the little itching worms kept very, very silent and fever was steeped in thought and dysentery bowed down his head, craw-craw started weeping, and the ulcer clicked his tongue in disgust, the rash frowned and the cold cried out for mercy.

Then mad women became elegant and madmen started to shave; and pregnant women delivered safely and nursing mothers walked about in happiness, the wizards repented and the witches begged for forgiveness and all the sacrificers and herbalists prostrated before my father.

But as I had told you, my friend, in the olden days, my mother was a hardened witch. She used to fly in the afternoon and fly in the night. She drank water from a human skull and she ate maize pap with the arm of a child. She used the leg of an old person to eat rice and the jaw bone of a strong man to drink gari.[7]

This is an ebullient prose style. Fagunwa heaps one absurd detail atop another until a highly humorous effect is achieved. He exaggerates, overstates, and belabors his point but does so with such imagination and wit that the reader cannot help but enjoy his verbosity. He is a master not only of rhetoric but of comedy. Significantly, Beier claims that the

true Yoruba flavour of Fagunwa's work lies not in the material he used, but in the language, in the manner and tone of his story telling. These are the elements to which the average Yoruba reader responds with delight: for Fagunwa has the humour, the rhetoric, the word play, the bizarre imagery that Yorubas like and appreciate in their language. He impresses the reader with his knowledge of classical Yoruba ("deep Yoruba" as the phrase goes) and he is as knowledgeable in proverbial expressions as an old oracle priest. Yet he is not content with that: he uses the language creatively and inventively, constantly adding to the traditional stock of imagery and enriching the language.[8]

The Yoruba writer whose works most closely resemble Fagunwa's is Amos Tutuola. Writing in eccentric English rather than classical Yoruba, Tutuola never manages to equal Fagunwa's eloquence or rhetorical finesse, but he does achieve similar humorous and bizarre effects by employing many of the narrative and descriptive techniques that Fagunwa popularized. For instance, Tutuola is often praised for the way he uses "the paraphernalia of modern life to give sharpness and immediacy to his imagery."[9] The classic example is his description of the terrible "red fish" in *The Palm-Wine Drinkard*:

> . . . its head was just like a tortoise's head, but it was as big as an elephant's head and it had over 30 horns and large eyes which surrounded the head. All these horns were spread out as an umbrella. It could not walk but was only gliding on the ground like a snake and its body was just like a bat's body and covered with long red hair like strings. It could only fly to a short distance, and if it shouted a person who was four miles away would hear. All the eyes which surrounded its head were closing and opening at the same time as if a man was pressing a switch on and off.[10]

Arresting images such as the umbrella-like horns and the electrically operated eyes seem quite original, but Fagunwa had used images of this sort in his first novel. Here is part of Fagunwa's description of Agbako, an evil spirit in *The Forest of a Thousand Daemons*:

> His head was long and large, the sixteen eyes being arranged around the base of his head, and there was no living man who could stare into those eyes without trembling, they rolled endlessly round like the face of a clock. His head was matted with hair, black as the hearth and very long, often swishing his hips as he swung his legs.[11]

Fagunwa's manner of describing monsters appears to have made a profound impression on Tutuola, leading him to strive for similar hallucinatory effects.

Occasionally Tutuola comes close to outright plagiarism. In his *Simbi and the Satyr of the Dark Jungle*, for example, Simbi's first encounter with the Satyr closely resembles Olowo-Aiye's meeting with Esu Kekere Ode ("Little Devil of the Ways") in Fagunwa's *Igbo Olodumare*. The monsters themselves are very much alike. Here is Fagunwa's Esu Kekere Ode:

> He wore no coat and he wore no trousers; he had no hat on his head and tied no cloth round his loins, for it was with leaves that the wretch covered his nakedness. He had only one eye and that was wide and round like a great moon. He had no nose at all because his eye was so much bigger than the ordinary bounds of an eye. His mouth was as wide as a man's palm and his teeth were like those of a lion, and these teeth were red as when a lion has just finished eating a meal of raw meat. The sprite's body was covered with hair like a garment and resembled that of a European dog. A long tuft of hair grew on top of his head. From his shoulder there hung a scourge and from his neck a great bag which filled one with fear. This bag was smeared all over with blood and on this blood was stuck the down of birds, while various medicines was attached to its sides. . . .[12]

Here is Tutuola's Satyr:

> . . . he did not wear neither coat nor trousers but he wore only an apron which was soaked with blood. Plenty of the soft feathers were stuck onto this apron. More than one thousand heads of birds were stuck to all over it. He was about ten feet tall and very strong, bold and vigorous. His head was full of dirty long hairs and the hairs were full up with refuses and dried leaves. The mouth was so large and wide that it almost covered the nose. The eyes were so fearful that a person could not be able to look at them for two times, especially the powerful illumination they were bringing out always. He wore plenty of juju-beads round his neck.[13]

Some of the descriptive details are different, but a great many are the same. Moreover, the action that follows is almost identical. Fagunwa's monster first interrogates the presumptuous earthling that has trespassed on his domain and then boasts of past conquests.

> "Who are you? What are you? What do you amount to? What do you rank as? What are you looking for? What do you want? What

are you looking at? What do you see? What are you considering? What affects you? Where are you coming from? Where are you going? Where do you live? Where do you roam? Answer me! Human being, answer me in a word! One thing is certain—you have got into trouble today, you have climbed a tree beyond its topmost leaves, you have fallen from a height into a well, you have eaten an unexpected poison, you have found a farm-plot full of weeds and planted ground-nuts in it. . . . You saw me and I saw you, you were approaching, and I was approaching, and yet you did not take to your heels. . . . Have you never heard of me? Has no one told you about me? The skulls of greater men than you are in my cooking pot and their backbones are in the corner of my room, while my seat is made from the breastbones of those who are thoughtless."[14]

Tutuola's less eloquent Satyr says the same:

"Who are you? What are you? where are you coming from? Where are you going? or don't you know where you are? Answer me! I say answer me now! . . . Certainly, you have put yourselves into the mouth of 'death'! You have climbed the tree above its leaves! you see me coming and you too are coming to me instead to run away for your lives!

By the way, have you not been told of my terrible deeds? And that I have killed and eaten so many persons, etc. who were even bold more than you do?"[15]

Both Fagunwa's hero and Tutuola's heroine respond by standing their ground and hurling back boasts of their own. In the strenuous wrestling match that ensues the monster is subdued.

It is encouraging to note that Tutuola and Fagunwa differ considerably in their description of this epic struggle and its aftermath. Such differences indicate that Tutuola is not merely translating Fagunwa and that he is sensitive to the demands of his own narrative. They also suggest that even when he follows Fagunwa most slavishly, he does so from memory rather than from a printed text, that instead of actually plagiarizing he vividly recreates what he best remembers from Fagunwa's books, knitting the spirit if not the substance of the most suitable material into the loose fibers of his yarn.

One should not conclude from these examples, however, that

Tutuola borrows only from Fagunwa. He also owes a great deal
to traditional Yoruba folk narratives. Ulli Beier states that
Fagunwa uses episodes and motifs from Yoruba folktales in his
books too, "but Fagunwa does not draw as heavily on Yoruba
folklore, as Tutuola . . . the stories [Tutuola] tells are in fact
more authentically Yoruba and traditional."[16] This leads one
to suspect that the manner in which Tutuola tells his stories has
been influenced as much by Yoruba oral tradition as by
Fagunwa and that the "true Yoruba flavour of Fagunwa's
work," which Beier says resides "in the manner and tone of
[Fagunwa's] story telling," also derives in large measure from
Yoruba oral tradition. Both writers appear to be greatly in debt
to the fireside raconteur.

Wole Soyinka, Nigeria's most versatile Yoruba author, has
neither Fagunwa's parochialism nor Tutuola's naiveté. Educated at universities in Nigeria and Britain, well-read in world
literature and *au courant* with the latest literary trends, Soyinka
is a sophisticated cosmopolitan who can draw upon sources of
inspiration which are not available to his less educated countrymen. His novel, *The Interpreters*, for example, certainly owes far
more to James Joyce and William Faulkner than it does to
Yoruba folktales. And his English is impeccable; one would
search his works in vain for the unconscious West Africanisms
and innocent barbarisms that crowd every page of Tutuola's
writing. Yet rhetorically Soyinka's prose is sometimes clearly
akin to Fagunwa's and Tutuola's. Take this monologue from
The Interpreters, for example:

> "Functional, spiritual, creative or ritualistic, Voidancy remains
> the one true philosophy of the true Egoist. For definition, ladies
> and gentlemen, let this suffice. Voidancy is not a movement of
> protest, but it protests: it is non-revolutionary, but it revolts.
> Voidancy—shall we say—is the unknown quantity. Voidancy
> is the last uncharted mine of creative energies, in its paradox
> lies the kernel of creative liturgy—in release is birth. I am no
> Messiah, and yet I cannot help but feel that I was born to
> fulfill this role, for in the congenital nature of my ailment lay the
> first imitations of my martyrdom and inevitable apotheosis. I was

born, with an emotional stomach. If I was angry, my stomach revolted; if I was hungry, it rioted; if I was rebuked, it reacted; and when I was frustrated, it was routed. It ran with anxiety, clammed up with tension, it was suspicious in examinations, and unpredictable in love. . . . I was often suspected of malingering and punishment was swift; and most empathic of the indications of an emotional stomach is the concomitant to a strong sense of injustice. Another influence on the shaping of my Voidant intro-version was the aunt of my childhood sweetheart, a sometime visitor to our home. She farted like a beast. And even more illu-minating was my own mother with the same affliction. She was a most religious farter. It was her boast, even as she neared the grave that God's voice was a wind which never failed to speak to her any day after evening prayers. And she called the household to wit-ness, and they said—Amen."[17]

Here Soyinka displays the same verbal ebullience and zany sense of humor that can be found in the works of Fagunwa and Tutuola. He likes to pile words up, make puns, repeat the same idea over and over again, varying it slightly each time. He revels in the ludicrous and bizarre, sometimes barely stopping short of the vulgar. He continually takes the reader by surprise, deluging him with unexpected images and unlikely events. And at times he allows himself to be carried away by his own metaphors. Here is another example:

> The rains of May become in July slit arteries of the sacrificial bull, a million bleeding punctures of the sky-bull hidden in convulsive cloud humps, black, overfed for this one event, nourished on horizon tops of endless choice grazing, distant beyond giraffe reach. Some competition there is below, as bridges yield right of way to lorries packed to the running-board, and the wet tar spins mirages of unspeed-limits to heroic cars and their cargoes find a haven below the precipice. The blood of earth-dwellers mingles with blanched streams of the mocking bull, and flows into currents eternally below earth.[18]

Who in Nigeria but a Yoruba poet brought up on the extrava-gant fantasies of Fagunwa and Tutuola would have had the audacity to write such florid prose?

It must be admitted, of course, that not every Yoruba prose

writer is as audacious, as exuberantly imaginative, as Soyinka, Tutuola and Fagunwa. T. M. Aluko is a case in point. Aluko's three novels are written in a rather quiet, colorless prose which resembles competent journalism. Instead of straining for exotic stylistic effects, Aluko is satisfied to describe fairly commonplace events in simple, straightforward English. There are moments in his novels, however, particularly in passages of dialogue between characters who are said to be speaking in Yoruba, when he employs the same sort of rhetoric, the same techniques of emphasis and exaggeration as we have seen in fiction by other Yoruba writers. Here is a scene in which a mother is trying to persuade her daughter to marry the man to whom she has been betrothed:

> "Joshua is our choice for you, Toro. Your spirits on both sides approved of him, Toro. He is your husband from heaven, Toro. You must marry him.
> "Joshua is a worthy man, Toro. Joshua is a wealthy man. He is strong. He descends from a line of kings and warriors. His father remains a legend in the annals of the tribe. He is very good looking, Toro. All the young women in the village feel flattered whenever he greets them. You must marry Joshua, my child.
> "Toro, you must heed my words," she said rather fiercely. "Toro, you must heed my words. Toro, I enjoin you to marry Joshua. By the womb in which I carried you for ten moons; by the great travail I underwent at your birth; by these breasts, now withered, on which I suckled you when you were helpless; by this back on which I carried you for nearly three years; by these knees on which I tended you; by the bush tracks that I trudged to the native doctors' farms when you lay between life and death. In the name of womanhood I entreat you to marry Joshua. In the name of motherhood I command you to marry Joshua."
> She paused for a long while after this. She coughed. It was a big burden off her chest. Then: "You will marry, Joshua, Toro?"
> No answer.
> "You will marry Joshua, won't you, Toro?"
> Two streams rolled down the girl's cheeks.
> "You will marry Joshua, Toro—or else you will face the consequences, Toro," she said fiercely.[19]

This vignette is splendidly orchestrated. It builds to a crescendo, eases off, then tightens up again. Repetition is used very skilfully to communicate the mother's emotion and to give the flavor of Yoruba speech.

Aluko is also capable of imitating the bombastic English sometimes employed by semi-educated Nigerians. In *One Man, One Wife* his hero, who bills himself as a "Public Letter Writer and Notary, Friend of the Illiterate, Advocate of the Oppressed," writes the following letter to the editor of a Lagos newspaper:

> Sir,
>
> Permit me a space in your widely and voraciously read journal to bring to the notice of the readers of your most widely read and voraciously digested newspaper domiciled in this great dependency of Nigeria some curious and wonderfully strange incidents and events that have been transpiring and occurring in one village in the District of Idasa, to wit Isolo.
>
> For many moons now the citizens of the ancient and historic town of Idasa have been subject and subjected to and exposed to the gross mercilessness and rank lawlessness and fiendish bloodthirstiness of a dangerous and violent gang and infernal team of nocturnal desperadoes, to wit a gang of thieves, burglars and robbers.
>
> The law-abiding citizens and inhabitants of this ancient town, to wit Idasa, have suffered irreparable loss from the malicious and murderous attacks of these nefarious workers in the dark, to wit the gang of thieves, burglars and robbers. [20]

Like other Yoruba novelists, Aluko seems to delight in wringing comedy out of verbal repetition and stylistic exaggeration.

Fustian rhetoric may well be a characteristic mode of Yoruba humor. And the novelists are certainly not the only ones to use it. The Hon. Adegoke Adelabu, a mercurial Ibadan politician who served as Leader of the Opposition in Nigeria's Western House of Assembly from 1956 until his death in 1958, was famous for his grandiloquence. In the early fifties he published a book entitled "*Africa in Ebullition*" *being a Handbook of Freedom for Nigerian Nationalists* in which he stated:

> This book derives many illustrations from astronomy, physics, chemistry, geography, engineering, agronomy and mathematics. It employs copiously the language of art, civics, biology, sociology,

music, literature and history. It is liberally spiced with Greek drama, Roman law, English idioms, American slangs, French logic, Indian mysticism and African folklore. It is an Ode to Liberty, a Guide to Nationalists, a Handbook of Freedom, a Grammar of Politics, a Revolutionary Manifesto, our Book of Revelation, an Encyclopaedia Nigeriana, the Voice of the People, a Challenge to Imperialism, an Indictment of Colonialism, an Abrogation of Gradualism, an Invitation to Youths, a Call to Arms, the Sacrament of Patriotism, a Psychoanalysis of the Nation, a Dissection of our Soul, an Answer to our Detractors, a Reaffirmation of Faith, a Plea for Unity, an Appeal for Understanding, a Rededication to the Struggle, a Bill of Rights, a Declaration of Independence, an Appreciation of Heroism, a Supplication for Sacrifices, an Atonement for Renegation, a Monument to Martyrdom and a Pact with Death. It is Versatility in Excelsis. I recommend it to those who dare. [21]

Adelabu's biographers [22] call this his "laundry list style," a term which could also be applied to portions of Fagunwa's writing. Adelabu's whole book is written in hyperbole. At one point he pauses to explain why:

The truth is that in these days of panegyrics, processions and hullaballoo the public is bombarded with an avalanche of propaganda by radio, hoardings, sky-signs, cinema, television, the written and the spoken word. The Struggles for Existence among Ideas and the Survival of the fittest among Creeds is of gigantic proportions and of unimaginable intensity. Truth stands no chance of receiving an audience unless it is clothed in Fashion, adumbrated in Novelty, adorned in Sensationalism and enthroned on the Pedestal of Originality. This is the Apologia for my literary style, suffused as it is with excessive exuberance. It is in accordance with the Spirit of the Age. In my artistic mood of translating my vision into language I pay no regard whatever to my public. If there, are among them, any hypersensitive prigs who take a fancy to a flat diet of evasive platitudes and equivocal plagiarisms I warn them, "Enter not into my brightly illuminated cellars. Here you will find no wines to suit your taste. Transfer your customs to some other drabmental Restaurant." I mean no harm by my literary persiflages! [23]

This rococo literary style, "suffused as it is with excessive exuberance," is typical of much Yoruba writing in English.

[165]

In sum, the examples quoted from Tutuola, Soyinka, Aluko and Adelabu suggest that one salient characteristic of Yoruba prose style in English is verbal ebullience. Yoruba writers exaggerate, embroider, reiterate and rant. Preferring to use ten words where one might suffice, they bombard their readers with bombast, goading them to laughter. Their bold inventiveness and keen appreciation of the ridiculous often find expression in bizarre incongruities of action and pyrotechnical poetic conceits. They seem to believe with Adelabu that "Truth stands no chance of receiving an audience unless it is clothed in Fashion, adumbrated in Novelty, adorned in Sensationalism and enthroned on the Pedestal of Originality." And the truth they seek to reveal is usually a comic or satiric truth, one which penetrates deeply with a light touch. But they mean no harm by their literary persiflages. They would much rather tickle than teach.

Most Ibo novelists who write in English employ a much quieter prose style. Eschewing the extravagant verbal antics of the Yorubas, they tend to favor a calm, graceful, proverb-studded idiom which resembles natural expression in their native tongue. The imagery, figures of speech and patterns of thought characteristic of communication in Ibo are rendered as faithfully as possible into English. Here is an example from the writings of Chinua Achebe, the first to use this simulated vernacular style:

Everybody at the kindred meeting took sides with Osugo when Okonkwo called him a woman. The oldest man present said sternly that those whose palm-kernels were cracked for them by a benevolent spirit should not forget to be humble. Okonkwo said he was sorry for what he had said, and the meeting continued.

But it was really not true that Okonkwo's palm-kernels had been cracked for him by a benevolent spirit. He had cracked them himself. Anyone who knew his grim struggle against poverty and misfortune could not say he had been lucky. If ever a man deserved his success, that man was Okonkwo. At an early age he had achieved fame as the greatest wrestler in all the land. That was not luck. At the most one could say that his *chi* or personal god was good. But the Ibo people have a proverb that when a man says yes his *chi* says yes also. Okonkwo said yes very strongly; so his *chi* agreed. And not only his *chi* but his clan too, because it judged a man by the work of his hands. [24]

Here there is none of the verbal excess one finds in Yoruba writing. The language is simple, clear, direct and evocative. The proverbs Achebe employs are not unnecessary embellishments but functional agents of characterization and culture description. It is clear that Achebe is more interested in communicating effectively than in overwhelming his readers with words.

Achebe has said:

The African writer should aim to use English in a way that brings out his message best without altering the language to the extent that its value as a medium of international exchange will be lost. He should aim at fashioning out an English which is at once universal and able to carry his peculiar experience. . . . I feel that the English language will be able to carry the weight of my African experience. But it will have to be a new English, still in full communion with its ancestral home but altered to suit its new African surroundings. [25]

To illustrate how he fashions out a universal English able to carry the weight of his African experience Achebe quotes a passage from his third novel, *Arrow of God*, in which a chief priest tells his son why he is being sent to a mission school:

"I want one of my sons to join these people and be my eye there. If there is nothing in it you will come back. But if there is something there you will bring home my share. The world is like a Mask dancing. If you want to see it well you do not stand in one place. My spirit tells me that those who do not befriend the white man today will be saying *had we known* tomorrow." [26]

Achebe then demonstrates that he could have written this passage in a different style:

I am sending you as my representative among those people—just to be on the safe side in case the new religion develops. One has to move with the times or else one is left behind. I have a hunch that those who fail to come to terms with the white man may well regret their lack of foresight. [27]

[167]

Achebe notes, "The material is the same. But the form of the one is *in character* and the other is not."[28] In order to achieve a style that is *in character* with the people and situations he describes in his village novels Achebe makes a deliberate effort to simulate in English the language used in Ibo villages. In other words he consciously fashions an Ibo prose style in English.

Many critics, African and non-African, have commented on the success of Achebe's efforts to Africanize (or, more exactly, to Iboize) English.[29] But even more convincing evidence of his success can be found in the fiction written by Ibos since the appearance of *Things Fall Apart* in 1958. Achebe's influence on the younger generation of Ibo novelists writing in English has been profound, especially in matters of style. First novelists such as Nkem Nwankwo, John Munonye, Flora Nwapa, Elechi Amadi, Clement Agunwa, and Edmund Uzodinma clearly constitute what may be termed a "School of Achebe" in African literature, for in telling stories of traditional Igbo village life they all employ stylistic techniques first introduced by Achebe.

The most obvious of these techniques is the use of traditional Ibo proverbs in narration and dialogue. Here are brief examples from each of Achebe's followers:

"No man can hold on to what Danda says. What Danda says has neither head nor tail."

There was laughter.

"It does not amuse me!" roared the Ikolo man. "It is long since Danda began pouring sand into our eyes."[30]

"Don't mind her good looks—even the millipede looks beautiful! Our people say that in a woman beauty of the body without that of the heart is nothing but sweetened poison. Do you know her latest deed?"[31]

Neighbours talked as they were bound to talk. They did not see the reason why Adizua should not marry another woman since, according to them, two men do not live together. To them Efuru was a man since she could not reproduce.[32]

The normal period of negotiations was a year, but Wigwe had rushed things. Each time Wagbara pointed out that a hen cannot lay eggs and hatch them on the same day, Wigwe had countered by saying that the slow-footed always fail in battle.[33]

"We are not like the caterpillar that clings tenaciously to the leaf when it is slim; but having fed fat, loosens his grips and falls to the earth to be food for hens. We are like soldier ants. We never lose our grip. We bite till our head goes into the struggle and we prefer to die rather than lose. Be like us."[34]

Ikilo had assured them, "We are ready to go with you even now and fight! The earth is an extensive mat on which everyone treads. If cow dung is thrown on its surface it will become unusable for everybody. The crime committed by Ndigwe traverses the whole of Igbo land."[35]

One also finds Ibo figures of speech transliterated into English. Nkem Nwankwo begins one of his chapters as follows:

The scorch season was dying. The happiest time of the year, the season for feasts, when men and women laughed with all their teeth and little boys, their mouths oily oily, ran about the lanes blowing the crops of chicken to make balloons.[36]

It is doubtful that Nwankwo would have employed expressions such as "season was dying," "laughed with all their teeth," and "mouths oil oily" had he not been impressed with Achebe's Iboization of English in *Things Fall Apart*.

In recent years several writers—notably Achebe, Nwankwo, Ike and Nzekwu—have ventured to include untranslated Ibo words in their novels. Usually these words can be understood in context and require no interpretation, but when used in great numbers they can easily baffle non-Ibo readers. In Nwankwo's *Danda* the reader is sometimes left to decipher passages such as the following:

The izaga dance is a perilous one, perilous for the dancer. For there are always among the spectators some malevolent dibias who would want to try out the power of a new ogwu by pulling the izaga down. To counter the nsi the izaga needed to be as strong as dried wood.[37]

To help the reader Nwankwo provides a glossary at the end of the book. This glossary helps Nwankwo too, for it frees him from

[169]

the responsibility of providing anthropological information in the narrative, information which would slow down the pace of the novel. Like other Ibo novelists who make use of Ibo words, Nwankwo appears to be more interested in communicating African concepts economically than in dazzling the reader with exotic vocabulary.

All the writers in the "school of Achebe" use an Iboized English to capture the spirit and flavor of Ibo village life. If their prose styles are similar, it is not because they all imitate Achebe but rather because they all base their styles on the same vernacular language. Achebe may have taught them how to render Ibo into English but he did not teach them how to render Ibo. The proverbs, figures of speech and Ibo words they employ are meant to simulate actual Ibo usage in the village. Fidelity to the common mother tongue is what matters most.

But what about the Ibo novelists who write of city life? Do they ever employ an Ibo prose style? Yes, some of them do but usually only to represent the speech of village characters who are purportedly speaking in Ibo. Chinua Achebe, in *A Man of the People*, has an old man scold his son in proverbs:

> "A mad man may sometimes speak a true word," said my father, "but, you watch him, he will soon add something to it that will tell you his mind is still spoilt. My son, you have again shown your true self. When you came home with a car I thought to myself: good, some sense is entering his belly at last. . . . But I should have known. So you really want to fight Chief Nanga! My son, why don't you fall where your pieces could be gathered? If the money he was offering was too small why did you not say so? Why did you not ask for three or four hundred? But then your name would not be Odili if you did that. No, you have to insult the man who came to you as a friend and—let me ask you something: Do you think he will return tomorrow to beg you again with two-fifty pounds? No, my son. You have lost the sky and you have lost the ground. . . ."[38]

Notice how each point the father makes is underscored by an appropriate proverb. Notice too that the proverbs are not repetitive. Each one carries a new idea in metaphor. Unlike the

Yoruba novelists who playfully reiterate a single idea by piling one metaphor upon another, Achebe uses metaphor to move from one idea to the next. He is more concerned with meaningful communication than with half-empty rhetoric.

Achebe is not the only novelist to employ an Ibo prose style in a non-village novel. Chukwuemeka Ike, in *Toads for Supper*, has his Ibo-speaking characters express themselves in a very similar fashion. Here, for example, is another father scolding his son:

> "Amobi. My words are few. You have painted my face and your mother's face with charcoal. I have always pulled your ears with my hand and warned you to beware of these township girls. I have begged you to put your sword in its sheath because one day you will be tired of lying down with a woman. I and your mother were anxious that you should marry quickly because we feared that young men of today find it difficult to control themselves. Nwakaego is waiting for you, just as the water in the broken pot waits for the dog to drink it. But I knew your mind was not on Nwakaego. You wanted someone who had gone to England to study, somebody who could speak English to you. Now that you have eaten the thing that has kept you awake let me watch you sleep! Now that you have fallen into the hands of those township girls who help the gods to kill, you will understand why I have been warning you to avoid women as you would avoid lepers. When a child eats a toad, it kills his appetite for meat." [39]

The proverbs add emphatic weight to each of the father's assertions. His speech is colorful but wise, not (as is so often the case in Yoruba novels) colorful and deliberately foolish.

Not all Ibo novelists who write in English make use of an Ibo prose style. Cyprian Ekwensi and Obi Egbuna are the outstanding exceptions. Of course, Ekwensi was brought up in Northern Nigeria and educated in Western Nigeria, Ghana and England, so he may not have had as much exposure to Ibo village life or as much experience speaking in the vernacular as other Ibo novelists have had. As for Egbuna, his years of law study in Britain may have so thoroughly Anglicized his writing style that he might find it extremely difficult to express himself in Iboized English. This is not to say that Ekwensi and Egbuna are incapable of employing an Ibo prose style. Perhaps in future novels they will make a concerted effort to differentiate artistically the speech of Ibo-speaking villagers from that of English-speaking city dwellers. So long as they know village Ibo they should be able to do so.

Onuora Nzekwu is an excellent example of an Ibo novelist who learned to write in an authentic Ibo prose style part way through his career. His first two novels, *Wand of Noble Wood* and *Blade Among the Boys*, were written in a stiff, formal prose occasionally spiced with quotations from Sir Walter Scott, Robert Southey and Shakespeare. Nzekwu did employ some Ibo words, proverbs and figures of speech in these novels, but he often vitiated their force by laboring to explain their meaning. And sometimes his tribal characters spoke in Oxonian English. Here is an uncle reprimanding his nephew:

> "How dare you speak of our traditional inheritance in that vein? Did I pay your fees at school for you to come back and call us names? Those things you call primitive sustained our ancestors, your parents and mine, for generations. Now you want to throw away all that our ancestors gave us, all the things that mark us distinctly as Ado." With a smile he added: "Those white men who call you monkeys are not very mistaken. How can they be when you, the literate ones among us, want everything of their way of life and reject everything that is your own without sorting out that which is good for you?" [40]

Achebe and Ike would have interlarded this speech with relevant Ibo proverbs. But Nzekwu did not learn to make effective use of Iboized English until his third novel, *Highlife for Lizards*. Consider the difference between the speech above and the one following, in which a man laments his wife's sterility:

> "It's a pity she's had no child. Yes, she's never even been pregnant, much less suffered a miscarriage. After all, what is needed in a seed yam is its crown. No one snaps his fingers without using a thumb. If only she'd had a child! What shall I tell my ancestors when I go to them? That while the dance lasted all I did was make preparations to join in it?" [41]

It is clear that by the time he wrote *Highlife for Lizards* Nzekwu had learned from his Ibo literary ancestors that "proverbs are the palm-oil with which words are eaten."

To sum up, the Ibo novelists quoted in this paper show a clear preference for a prose style in English which simulates natural expression in their native tongue. By introducing traditional Ibo proverbs, idioms, images and words into their fiction, they produce a convincing, in-depth portrait of traditional Ibo society. Unlike the Yoruba novelists who revel in fantasy and comic exaggeration, the Ibo novelists tend to favor realism and sober moral truths. Instead of verbal ebullience they prize verbal economy, for they would far rather instruct than entertain.[42]

From this investigation we may conclude that today there are at least two distinctive tribal prose styles in African literature in English, the Yoruba and the Ibo. That there will be many more tomorrow seems certain. Chinua Achebe once said that "the price a world language must be prepared to pay is submission to many different kinds of use."[43] In Africa the English language is already beginning to pay that price.

NOTES

1 Robert Plant Armstrong, "The Characteristics and Comprehension of a National Literature—Nigeria," in *Proceedings of a Conference on African Languages and Literatures held at Northwestern University, April 28-30, 1966*, ed. Jack Berry *et al.* (n.p., n.d.), pp. 117-32.

2 The concept of ethnicity in African literature is discussed by Armstrong (*Ibid.*, pp. 120f.), who states that "any work executed by an individual informed by the unique values, perceptions, esthetics, and the whole system of social, political, and economic structures of an ethnic group—black or white, Moslem or Christian, educated or nearly illiterate—contributes to and defines the literature of that group." The tribalist critic must therefore study the tribe's entire literature.

3 One anthropologist who has approached African literature tribally is Austin J. Shelton. See, e.g., his paper "The Articulation of Traditional and Modern in Igbo Literature," *The Conch*, 1. No. 1 (1969), 30–52.

4 Wole Soyinka has published a translation of Fagunwa's first novel, *Ogboju Ode Ninu Igbo Irunmale*, under the title *The Forest of a Thousand Daemons: A Hunter's Saga* (London, 1968). Portions of this translation appeared in *Black Orpheus*, No. 15 (August 1964), pp. 5–7, and *Black Orpheus*, No. 19 (March 1966), pp. 17–21. Other translations of excerpts from Fagunwa's fiction are: "The Bold Hunter in the Forest of Zombis," trans. A. Akiwowo, *Odu*, No. 9 (September 1963), pp. 35–37; "The Beginning of Olowo Aiye," trans. Bakare Gbadamosi and Ulli Beier, *Odu*, No. 9 (September 1963), pp. 31–34; "The Forest of the Lord," trans. E. C. Rowlands, in *A Selection of African Prose* (2. *Written Prose*), ed. Wilfred Whiteley (London, 1964), pp. 69–84.

5 Soyinka, *Forest of a Thousand Daemons*, p. 9.

6 Ulli Beier, "D. O. Fagunwa: A Yoruba Novelist," *Black Orpheus*, No. 17 (June 1965), p. 53.

7 *Odu*, No. 9 (September 1963), p. 33.

8 Beier, "D. O. Fagunwa," p. 52.

9 Gerald Moore, *Seven African Writers* (London, 1962), p. 43.

10 Amos Tutuola, *The Palm-Wine Drinkard and His Dead Palm-Wine Tapster in the Deads' Town* (New York, 1953), pp. 79–80.

11 *Black Orpheus*, No. 15 (August 1964), p. 6.

12 Wilfred Whiteley, ed., *A Selection of African Prose* (2. *Written Prose*) (London, 1964), pp. 73–74.

13 Amos Tutuola, *Simbi and the Satyr of the Dark Jungle* (London, 1955), pp. 73–74.

14 Whiteley, *African Prose*, pp. 74–75.

15 Tutuola, *Simbi*, p. 75.

16 Beier, pp. 52–56.

17 Wole Soyinka, *The Interpreters* (London, 1965), p. 71.

18 *Ibid.*, p. 155.

19 T. M. Aluko, *One Man, One Wife* (Lagos, 1959), pp. 107–08.

20 *Ibid.*, p. 123.

21 Adegoke Adelabu, *"Africa in Ebullition"* being a Handbook of Freedom for Nigerian Nationalists (Ibadan, n.d.), pp. 24–25.

22 George Jenkins and Kenneth Post, *The Prince of Power* (forthcoming).

23 Adelabu, *"Africa in Ebullition,"* p. 13.

24 Chinua Achebe, *Things Fall Apart* (London, 1958), pp. 22–23.

25 Chinua Achebe, "English and the African Writer," *Transition*, No. 18 (1965), pp. 29–30.

26 *Ibid.*

27 *Ibid.*

28 *Ibid.*

29 Gerald Moore, "English Words, African Lives," *Présence Africaine*, No. 54 (1965), pp. 90–101; Ezekiel Mphahlele, "The Language of African Literature," *Harvard Educational Review*, 34 (Spring 1964), 298–305; Eldred Jones, "Language and Theme in *Things Fall Apart*," *Review of English Literature*, 5 (October 1964), 39–43; and Gareth Griffiths, "Language and Action in the Novels of Chinua Achebe," *African Literature Today*, No. 5 (1971), pp. 88–105.

30 Nkem Nwankwo, *Danda* (London, 1964), p. 29.

31 John Munonye, *The Only Son* (London, 1966), p. 122.

32 Flora Nwapa, *Efuru* (London, 1966), p. 23.

33 Elechi Amadi, *The Concubine* (London, 1966), p. 168.

34 Clement Agunwa, *More Than Once* (London, 1967), p. 119.

35 E. C. C. Uzodinma, *Our Dead Speak* (London, 1967), p. 64.

36 Nwankwo, *Danda*, p. 81.

37 Nwankwo, p. 22.

38 Chinua Achebe, *A Man of the People* (London, 1966), p. 135.

39 Chukwuemeka Ike, *Toads for Supper* (London, 1965), p. 120.

40 Onuora Nzekwu, *Blade Among the Boys* (London, 1962), p. 114.

41 Onuora Nzekwu, *Highlife for Lizards* (London, 1965), p. 54.

42 In a letter written after reading this essay Peter Young suggested that perhaps the difference between Yoruba and Ibo prose styles may be partly the result of differences in tribal social structure. The Yoruba hierarchical kingship system may have encouraged ornamented oratory while Ibo democracy fostered direct but figurative communication. I think this is an intriguing idea which should be investigated by scholars familiar with styles of oral discourse in both cultures. Another related hypothesis which warrants further study is the notion that Yoruba rhetoric is essentially an urban phenomenon, while Ibo rhetoric is the type that tends to be produced in rural areas. The urban speaker has to be an entertainer to gain attention in a large crowd. He must be a performer first and a communicator second; in fact, performance is the essence of oral communication. In a small village community, on the other hand, the message is more important than the mode of delivery. Here communication is placed first, performance second; indeed, communication is the essense of oral performance. Since the Yoruba tend to be an urban people and the Ibo a rural people, it is not surprising that their rhetorical preferences differ considerably. One hopes that African scholars will begin to take an interest in this field of research and tell us more than we currently know about the ethnography of speaking in various African communities.

43 Achebe, "English and the African Writer," p. 29.

INDEX